Daniel Plunkett

"Many false prophets will arise and
lead many astray."
JESUS CHRIST

LEARN TO DISCERN

Recognizing False Teachings In the
Christian Church Today

LEARN TO DISCERN

Recognizing False Teachings In the Christian Church Today

Daniel Plunkett

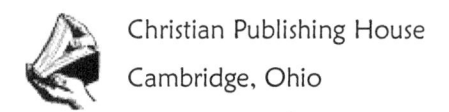

Christian Publishing House
Cambridge, Ohio

Christian Publishing House
Professional Conservative Christian
Publishing of the Good News!

CPH Since 2005

Copyright © 2018 Daniel Plunkett

All rights reserved. Except for brief quotations in articles, other publications, book reviews, and blogs, no part of this book may be reproduced in any manner without prior written permission from the publishers. For information, write, support@christianpublishers.org

Unless otherwise stated, Scripture quotations are from the Updated American Standard Version (UASV) Copyright © 2018 by Christian Publishing House

LEARN TO DISCERN: Recognizing False Teachings In the Christian Church Today

Authored by Daniel Plunkett

ISBN-13: **978-1-949586-00-8**

ISBN-10: **1-949586-00-6**

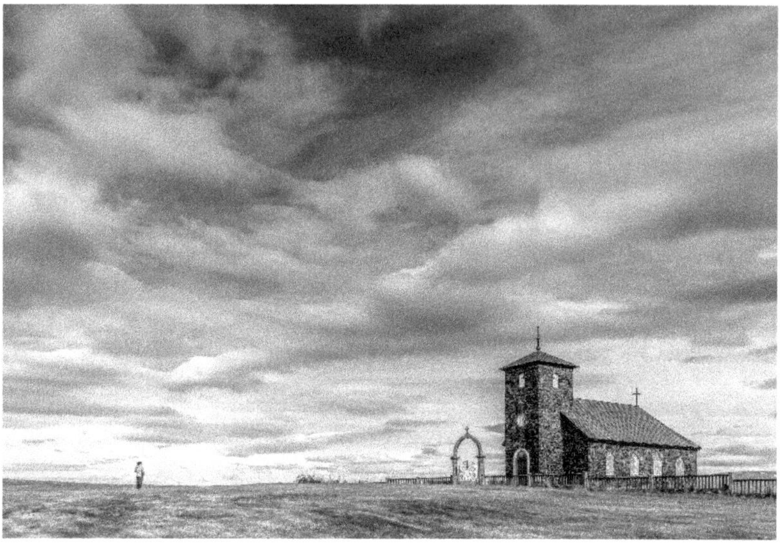

Table of Contents

FORWARD 1
   Basics in Biblical Interpretation 5
   Biblical Interpretation Explained in Greater Detail 5
   Some Scriptures to Consider 7
INTRODUCTION 10
CHAPTER 1 Christian Media 11
   Word of Faith 101 13
   Origins of the Word of Faith Movement 19
   The Dake Reference Bible 21
CHAPTER 2 Kenneth Copeland 23
CHAPTER 3 The Prosperity Preachers 35
CHAPTER 4 Personal Experience with the Word of 47
   Some Thoughts on Faith Healing 51
   Slain in the Spirit 62
   Kundalini? 66
   Some Thoughts on the Charismatic Movement 67
   Have the Sign Gifts Ceased or Not? 69
CHAPTER 5 Error Gives Birth to Error: The New Apostolic Reformation 86
   The Song of Seduction 92
   Sid Roth 99
   The Supremacy of "Experience" 101
   The Sufficiency of Scripture 101
   A Look at the "Prophets" 103
   Unity at Any Cost 105
   What Does It All Mean? 106
   What about the Fruit? 108
CHAPTER 6 Why Does God Allow False Teachers? 109

EXCURSION APOCALYPTIC END TIMES: Exposing "the Man of Lawlessness" 111
    Some Final Thoughts 130
    What about Other Groups? 130
    Ten Tips for Discernment 131
  CONCLUSION After Thoughts 135
  APPENDIX 1 Partial List of Modern False Teachers; 137
  APPENDIX 2: Commonly Misused Scriptures 140
  Bibliography 143

FORWARD

We live in an age where *tolerance* is highly valued but is tolerance always a good thing? For Christians, the answer is a resounding *no*! As believers, one thing we should *never* tolerate is people claiming to speak for God, while blatantly misrepresenting Him. Today, Christians are chided to *judge not*, as if discernment were a distasteful thing. We are taught to tolerate unbiblical doctrines and to agree to disagree on such matters. However, it is absolutely wrong to hold hands and sing *Kum Ba Yah* with folks who promote teachings contrary to biblical doctrines regarding the Trinity, the nature of God, man, salvation, etc. Yet, that is exactly what is happening in the modern church. Pastors who should - and do - know better, are not speaking out against those who teach falsely, and as a result, their congregations are blindly swallowing heresy, without rebuke or warning from their leaders. We are about to discuss how there are some things that are okay to disagree on, however, there are certain truths that absolutely *cannot be compromised*, lest doctrinal confusion can morph into a false *gospel*. Heresy has crept into mainstream Christianity so smoothly that most people can't even recognize it. Those who teach such heresies are *not* our brothers and sisters in Christ; they are *false teachers*, preaching a *false gospel*, often under demonic influence, and the Bible has harsh words for them, and for those who would follow them! False teachers are a very serious matter. Those who are already saved won't lose their salvation by listening to them, but they are often led to embrace false hope (and inevitable discouragement) based on empty promises. Those who are unsaved will be steered towards a false gospel that cannot save them and remain eternally lost unless someone tells them the truth. Therefore, today, more than ever, it is vital that we *learn to discern* truth from error.

Heresy: (*hairesis*) Heresy literally means "a choice or an option." A destructive *choice* or *option* of a school of thought or a teaching of a false religious sect, faction, or a teacher. Heresy is a doctrinal view or position that is accepted by a so-called "Christian" group(s), sect(s), or teacher(s) that is unbiblical, i.e., a false teaching, untrue doctrine that is foreign to what the Bible authors meant by the words that they used. These unbiblical views or positions were not merely indifferent or harmless but rather were destructive to the faith. – 2 Peter 2:1.

A **heretic** would be a false religious sect, faction, or a teacher who holds a destructive school of thought or a teaching that is unbiblical, i.e., a false teaching, untrue doctrine that is foreign to what the Bible authors meant by the words that they used.

Heterodox is generally defined as a doctrinal view or position "contrary to or different from an acknowledged standard, a traditional form, or an established religion: unorthodox, unconventional, holding unorthodox opinions or doctrines."[1] However, herein, this author would rather limit heterodox to a doctrinal view or position that is contrary to the Word of God, i.e., what the authors meant by the words that they used.

Deviation from God's Word (what the author meant) is what determines a heresy not some church or church tradition. For our purposes, some clarification is required to understand how these terms are used by mainstream evangelical Christians. Dogma could refer to any group or denomination's foundational beliefs. In this discussion, dogma will refer to what evangelical Christians refer to as Reformed theology:

- **The Study of the Father** (power, greatness, nearness, goodness, revelation, absolute inerrancy of Scripture)
- **The Study of the Son** (Christological method, deity of Christ, humanity of Christ, person of Christ, virgin birth, the atonement of Christ)
- **The Study of the Holy Spirit** (person, work)[2]
- **The Study of Humanity** (origin, image, constitutional nature)
- **The study of Sin** (nature, source, results, magnitude)
- **The study of Salvation** (conceptions, antecedent, beginning, continuation, completion, means, and extent)
- **Inerrancy of Scripture** (The original sixty-six books of the Bible are without error or fault in all its teaching)

These are the foundational doctrines of our faith. This is not to say that there are some things that the Bible teaches us is not important. Truly, everything the Bible teaches us is important or otherwise, it would not be in the Bible. Just as all sin is sinful; however, the Bible itself and God call some sins gross sin, qualifying them as being more heinous. Certainly, no rational person would see stealing a piece of candy from a store as being equal to committing aggravated murder or rape. Therefore, it is also true

---

[1] Inc Merriam-Webster, *Merriam-Webster's Collegiate Dictionary.* (Springfield, MA: Merriam-Webster, Inc., 2003).

[2] The Holy Spirit and Jesus (http://tiny.cc/sibwqy) The Holy Spirit and the Apostles (http://tiny.cc/vgbwqy) The Holy Spirit in the First Century and Today (http://tiny.cc/pabwqy) The Holy Spirit and the Apostolic Church (http://tiny.cc/3fbwqy) The Holy Spirit and the World (http://tiny.cc/ffbwqy) The Work of the Holy Spirit (http://tiny.cc/sjbwqy) How Are We to Understand the Indwelling of the Holy Spirit? (http://tiny.cc/1mbwqy) How Do We Receive the Holy Spirit Today? (http://tiny.cc/lel7qy) Are Answers to Our Prayerful Requests Absolutely Guaranteed? (http://tiny.cc/6yk7qy) Is Foreknowledge Compatible with Free Will? (http://tiny.cc/1i1isy)

that some doctrinal positions and views are more significant than others, but all are important. Surely, we would say one is a heretic if they have the heterodox teaching of **not confessing** the coming of Jesus Christ in the flesh. Another heterodox teaching would be the **rejection** of the ransom sacrifice that of the shed blood of Jesus Christ, which pays or covers over the sins of repentant ones who accept Jesus Christ, delivering them from the sin and death. However, we would **not say** one is a heretic if they have the unbiblical teaching that the earth was created in seven literal days over the biblical teaching that the creation days were creation periods. The same holds true on the different views of foreknowledge.

A heterodox doctrinal view or position that is a false teaching, an untrue doctrine that is foreign to what the Bible authors meant by the words that they used. These unbiblical views or positions that are foundational, more significant are not merely indifferent or harmless but rather are destructive to the faith. These unbiblical views or positions that are foundational would be on such doctrines as inerrancy of Scripture, atonement, sanctification, salvation, among others, if foreign to what the Bible authors meant by the words that they used. These heretical teachings on foundational doctrines of the faith can lead people away from the truths of Scripture and possibly towards eternal destruction. Such heresies are destructive, indeed.

The purpose of this book in what follows is to shine the light of Scripture upon some of the most commonly taught heresies corrupting the church today. Once again, there are some things that do not rise to the level of heresy that we may disagree on. The destructive heresies that I hope to alert you to are those foundational, more significant doctrinal positions or views. Knowing how to study the Bible and how to interpret the Bible are essential if we are to avoid teaching unbiblical doctrinal positions or views ourselves.

Sadly, survey after survey over the last 35 years has shown that 90+ percent of Christians today are in the same position as what Paul had said to the Hebrew Christians. "For in view of the time you ought to be teachers, you have need again for someone to teach you from the beginning the elementary things of the words of God, and you have come to need milk and not solid food." (Heb. 5:12) On this verse, Thomas D. Lea wrote, "First, he said, 'You've been Christians long enough to be teachers, but you still need instruction in the ABCs.' They should have been able to pass on their basic understanding of the Christian message to others. Instead, they needed a good review of the elementary matters themselves. Not only had they failed to move forward in their understanding; they had lost their grasp of the **elementary truths of God's word.** 'If the dark things do not become plain then the plain things will become dark' (Thomas Hewitt). Second, these believers were in need of **milk, not solid food!** The term *milk* represents a beginning level of instruction for Christians. The term solid food describes advanced instruction. Both the milk phase and the solid food phase were important and essential. However, someone who never reached the solid food stage was seriously defective. ... The writer of Hebrews was concerned that his readers should be showing signs of Christian maturity. They were still caught up in issues only 'baby' Christians found to be important."[3] Do not be troubled by these words, as to biblical illiteracy among the Christians today, the church and its leaders bear most of the responsibility by far, with some going to the churchgoer as well.

Joshua 1:8-9 Updated American Standard Version (UASV)

[8] This Book of the Law shall not depart from your mouth, but you shall **meditate** on it **day and night**, so that you may be careful to do according to all that is written in it; for then you will make your way prosperous, and then **you will have good success**. [9] Have I not commanded you? Be strong and courageous! Do not be afraid, and do not be dismayed, for Jehovah your God is with you wherever you go."

We see that we need to **meditate** on God's Word **day and night** (See also Ps. 1:1-3). The day and night are really hyperbole for reading it every day. The Hebrew word behind meditate (*haghah*) can be rendered "mutter." In other words, as we read, we are to read in an undertone, slightly out load, like muttering to oneself. The process of hearing the words increases our retention of the material dramatically. As Bible students, we read to understand and remember what we read, and we are obligated to share this good news with others. Gesenius' Hebrew and Chaldee Lexicon (translated by S. Tregelles, 1901, p. 215) say of haghah: "Prop[erly] to speak with oneself, murmuring and in a low voice, as is often done by those who are musing."[4]

The last phrase in verse 8, "you will have good success" can be rendered to "act with insight." How was Joshua to acquire this ability "to act with insight"? He was to meditate on God's Word day and night. What is the equation of Joshua 1:8? If Joshua were to read meditatively (in an undertone) from God's Word daily, applying it in his life, he would be able to act with insight, resulting in his prospering. Of course, the prospering is not financial gain. It is a life of joy and happiness in an age of difficult times. It is avoiding the pitfalls that those in the world

---

[3] Thomas D. Lea, *Hebrews, James*, vol. 10, Holman New Testament Commentary (Nashville, TN: Broadman & Holman Publishers, 1999), 95–96.

[4] See also Psalm 35:28; 37:30; 71:24; Isaiah 8:19; 33:18.

around us suffer daily. Moreover, it does not mean that we are to prosper or be successful in an absolute sense because bad things happen to good people. We must add the qualifier, "generally speaking," if we follow God's Word we will have success.

Basics in Biblical Interpretation

Step 1: What is the historical setting and background for the author of the book and his audience? Who wrote the book? When and under what circumstances was the book written? Where was the book written? Who were the recipients of the book? Did you find anything noteworthy about the place of the recipients? What is the theme of the book? What was the purpose for writing the book?

Step 2a: What would this text mean to the original audience? (The meaning of a text is what the author meant by the words that he used, as should have been understood by his readers.)

Step 2b: If there are any words in this section that one does not understand, or that stand out as interesting words that may shed some insight on the meaning, look them up in a word dictionary, such as *Mounce's Complete Expository Dictionary of Old and New Testament Words*.

Step 2c: After reading this section from the three Bible translations, do a word study and write down what you think the author meant. Then, pick up a trustworthy commentary, like Holman Old or New Testament commentary volume, and see if you have it correct.

Step 3: Explain the original meaning in one or two sentences, preferably one. Then, take the sentence or two and place it in a short phrase.

Step 4: Now, consider their circumstances, the reason for it being written, what it meant to them, and consider examples from today that would be similar to that time, which would fit the pattern of meaning. What **implications** can be drawn from the original meaning?

Step 5: Find the pattern of meaning, the "thing like these," and consider how it could apply in modern life. How should individual Christians today live out the implications and principles?

Biblical Interpretation Explained in Greater Detail

Step 1: What is the historical setting and background for the author of the book and his audience? Who wrote the book? When and under what circumstances was the book written? Where was the book written? Who were the recipients of the book? Did you find anything noteworthy about the place of the recipients? What is the theme of the book? What was the purpose for writing the book? The first step is observation, to get as close to the original text as possible. If you do not read Hebrew or Greek; then, two or three literal translations are preferred (ESV, NASB, and UASV).[5] The above Bible background information may seem daunting, but it can all be found in the Holman Bible Handbook or the Holman Illustrated Bible Dictionary.

Step 2a: What would this text have meant to the original audience? (The meaning of a text is what the author meant by the words that he used, as should have been understood by his readers.) Once someone has an understanding of step 1, read and reread the text in its context. In most Bibles, there are indentations or breaks where the subject matter changes. Look for the indentations that are before and after the text and read and read that whole section from three literal translations. If there are no indentations, read the whole chapter and identify where the subject matter changes.

Step 2b: If there are any words in the section that one does not understand, or that stands out as interesting words that may shed some insight on the meaning, look them up in a word dictionary, such as *Mounce's Complete Expository Dictionary of Old and New Testament Words*. For example, if the text was Ephesians 5:14, ask what Paul meant by "sleeper" in verse 14. If it was Ephesians 5:18, what did Paul mean by using the word "debauchery" in relation to "getting drunk with wine." I would recommend *Mounce's Complete Expository Dictionary of Old and New Testament Words* by William D. Mounce (Sep 19, 2006) Do not buy the Amazon Kindle edition until they work out a difficulty. If you have Logos Bible Software, it would be good to add this book if it did not come with the package.

Step 2c: After reading the section from the three Bible translations, do a word study and write down what you think the author meant. Then, pick up a trustworthy commentary, like Holman Old or New Testament commentary volume, checking to see if you have it correct. It can be more affordable to buy one volume each time a project is assigned so that it is spread out over time. If one cannot afford each volume of these commentary sets, Holman has a one-volume commentary on the entire Bible. Also, check with the pastor of your church because he may allow you to take a volume home for the assignment.

Step 3: Explain the original meaning in one or two sentences, preferably one. Then, take the sentence or two and place it in a short phrase. If you look in the Bible for Ephesians chapter five, you will find

---

[5] http://www.uasvbible.org/

verses 1-5 or 6 are marked off as a section, and the phrase that captures the sense of the meaning, is "imitators of God." Then, verses 6-16 of that same chapter can be broken down to "light versus darkness" or "walk like children of light."

Step 4: Consider their circumstances, the reason for it being written, what it meant to them, and consider examples from our day that would be similar to the time they lived, which would fit the pattern of meaning. What **implications** can be drawn from the original meaning? Part of this fourth step ensures the Bible student stays within the pattern of the original meaning to determine any implications for the reader.

An example would be the admonition that Paul gave the Ephesian congregation at 5:18, "do not get drunk with wine." Was Paul talking about beer that existed then, too? Surely, he was not explicitly referring to whiskey, which would be centuries before it was invented. Yes, Paul refers to the others because they provide implications that can be derived from the original meaning.

Step 5: Find the pattern of meaning, the "thing like these," and consider how it could apply in modern life. How should individual Christians today live out the implications and principles?[6]

Some Scriptures to Consider

2 Timothy 4:3-4 Updated American Standard Version (UASV)

[3] For there will be a time when they will not put up with sound teaching, but in accordance with their own desires, they will accumulate teachers for themselves to have their ears tickled,[7] [4] and will turn away their ears from the truth and will turn aside to myths. [4] and will turn away their ears from the truth and will turn aside to myths. [5] But you, be sober-minded[8] in all things, endure hardship, do the work of an evangelist, fulfill your ministry.

Matthew 7:22-23 Updated American Standard Version (UASV)

[22] On that day many will say to me, 'Lord, Lord, did we not prophesy in your name, and cast out demons in your name, and do many mighty

---

[6] Edward D. Andrews, *HOW TO STUDY YOUR BIBLE: Rightly Handling the Word of God* (Cambridge, OH: Christian Publishing House, 2017), 178-80.

[7] Or *to tell them what they want to hear*

[8] **Sober Minded**: (Gr. *nepho*) This denotes being sound in mind, to be in control of one's thought processes and thus not be in danger of irrational thinking, 'to be sober-minded, to be well composed in mind.'–1 Thessalonians 5:6, 8; 2 Timothy 4:5; 1 Peter 1:13; 4:7; 5:8

works in your name?' ²³ And then I will declare to them, 'I never knew you; depart from me, you who practice **lawlessness**.'

We will see as we move forward how there are many people today claiming to do miracles and cast out demons in the name of Jesus, yet they are not operating in the name of the biblical, true Jesus, a very serious sin.

Matthew 24:24 Updated American Standard Version (UASV)

²⁴ For false Christs and false prophets will arise and will show great signs and wonders, so as to mislead, if possible, even the **chosen ones**.[9]

Throughout our discussion, keep this verse in mind as we examine how cleverly false teachers will deceive people with the appearance of miracles, some real; some fraudulent. Remember that the enemy does have some power to mimic certain miracles of God.

2 Peter 2:1-3 Updated American Standard Version (UASV)

2 But false prophets also arose among the people, just as there will also be false teachers among you, who will secretly introduce destructive heresies, even denying the Master who bought them, bringing swift destruction upon themselves. ² Many will follow their **acts of shameless conduct**,[10] and because of them the way of the truth will be spoken of abusively; ³ and in their greed they will exploit you with false words; their judgment from long ago is not idle, and their destruction is not asleep.

In this passage, Peter is making it clear that there will be false prophets amongst the church, and many will follow in their ways. In verse 2, Peter asserts that it will be the sensuality of the false prophets that will appeal to people. Bear in mind how many people today are following certain preachers based on promises of health, wealth and material things. These are not spiritual interests; they are carnal.

2 Thessalonians 2:8-12 Updated American Standard Version (UASV)

⁸ Then the lawless one will be revealed, whom the Lord Jesus will do away with by the spirit of his mouth, and wipe out by the appearance[11] of

---

[9] Or *the elect*

[10] Or *their sensuality; their licentious ways; their brazen conduct*

[11] **Appearing**: (Gr. *epiphaneia*) It literally means "a shining forth," which was used to refer to a divine being becoming visible to humans. *Epiphaneia* is used in the NT to refer to Jesus first coming to the earth and his second coming as well. – 2 Thess. 2:8; 1 Tim. 6:14; 2 Tim. 1:10; 4:1, 8.

his coming,[12] [9] namely, the one whose coming[13] is in accordance with the activity of Satan, with all power and signs and false wonders, [10] and with every unrighteous deception[14] for those who are perishing, because they did not receive the love of the truth so as to be saved. [11] For this reason God is sending upon them a powerful delusion[15] so that they will believe the lie, [12] in order that they all may be judged because they did not believe the truth but took pleasure in unrighteousness.

Again, we see how in the last days, Satan will seduce and deceive with signs and wonders, those folks who choose not to believe biblical truths but prefer a false message that appeals to the flesh.

---

[12] **Presence; Coming:** (Gr. *parousia*) The Greek word literally means," which is derived from *para*, meaning "with," and *ousia*, meaning "being." It denotes both an "arrival" and a consequent "presence with." Depending on the context, it can mean "presence," "arrival," "appearance," or "coming." In some contexts, this word is describing the presence of Jesus Christ in the last days, i.e., from his ascension in 33 C.E. up unto his second coming, with the emphasis being on his second coming, the end of the age of Satan's reign of terror over the earth. We do not know the day nor the hours of this second coming. (Matt 24:36) It covers a marked period of time with the focus on the end of that period. – Matt. 24:3, 27, 37, 39; 1 Cor. 15:23; 16:17; 2 Cor. 7:6-7; 10:10; Php 1:26; 2:12; 1 Thess. 2:19; 3:13; 4:15; 5:2.
[13] See note on 2:8.
[14] Lit *seduction*
[15] Or *a deluding influence*; Lit *an operation of deceit*

INTRODUCTION

Above are some scriptures that most believers are well acquainted with. They've heard them time and again, to the point where they are taken for granted. Even a casual glance at what is happening in today's church will show that these verses desperately need to be heeded, and yet they are not. There is a vast wave of deception taking place and most people are unaware of it. Many Christians attend good churches where solid biblical teaching is offered, and yet they go home and listen to false teachers on TV and radio without even realizing it. So, let's look at what's being promoted within what I like to call *Popular Christianity.* And I must say I've reached the sad conclusion that two of the most dangerous places for today's believers are Christian TV and the Christian bookstores. As we go forward will see that much of what's being promoted by these outlets do not represent Biblical Christianity at all, no matter how popular it is. And it must be noted that the gospel of scripture has *never* been popular in the least! Therefore, I'm aware that what I'm going to say going forward is going to offend some folks, but it needs to be said and examined in the light of scripture.

I would challenge you to consider and refer to the above scriptures as we move along and think about how they relate to the church today. Too many people think they are above deception, whereas scripture warns that false teachers *will* deceive people with signs and wonders, and by telling them just what they want to hear; two key points to keep in mind. I hope as we proceed, you will come to agree that the ability to discern truth from error is needed now more than ever….

CHAPTER 1 Christian Media

I mentioned Christian media, so that's where we'll start. There are many religious TV networks out there. TBN and Daystar are two of the most well-known and popular. Most people don't know that both of those networks, along with many others are run by proponents of something called *Word of Faith* theology with a distinct purpose of promoting such beliefs. TBN was founded by Paul and Jan Crouch, both staunch Word of Faith advocates. Today it is in the hands of Matt Crouch, still promoting the same beliefs. Daystar is run by Marcus and Joni Lamb, also dedicated promoters of Word of Faith beliefs. Other popular networks, such as God TV, are run by proponents of the *New Apostolic Reformation,* another unbiblical movement we will also discuss. It would hardly be surprising if many readers have no idea what Word of Faith is. I know firsthand of people who are listening to Word of Faith teachers on an almost daily basis yet have never heard the term or know what it means. So, we need to examine that belief system and ask if it lines up with the Word of God. Once we do that, we'll go more in depth as to who is teaching these doctrines and the names may surprise you.

Should you choose to switch on TBN or Daystar, etc. at any given time, you are likely to hear similar messages regardless of who's speaking. You'll hear that it is never God's will for you to be sick; that it is always His will to heal. You'll hear that God desires for all His children to walk in abundant financial prosperity. You may hear that you don't even need to pray for illnesses to be healed; use your authority as a believer to command the illness to leave. *(And never pray, if it be Thy will, as that shows a lack of faith!)* You'll hear that if you are desiring some outcome in your life, you just need to "call those things that be not as though they are;" that you can speak your desires into existence. Name it and claim it. You will hear that if you tithe, and give above and beyond the tithe, God will bless you with wealth. Yes, you will hear all these things said, along with *(out of context)* scriptures to support them.

And if you're like many people, you may have found that what goes on in your real life bears little or no resemblance to the "abundant life" you've been hearing about on TV. And yet, if you're like many people, you keep trusting that the things you've been told are true. Perhaps you've heard your favorite TV preachers explain to you that if you have not been healed, or have not received that financial breakthrough, then it is most likely because you lack faith, or haven't confessed some secret sin. And if you're like some people, you may find yourself in a train wreck of shattered faith, since none of the promises you've been clinging to ever seem to manifest.

And if you're like many people, you may just be waking up to the fact that much of what you've been led to believe simply is not true. There's a reason for that, and that reason is that a huge percentage of what you hear on Christian TV is not true. In fact, it even contradicts the Bible, yet these televangelists are so smooth at making lies sound biblical that millions are being deceived.

The gospel is indeed good news, but not every promise in scripture will come to pass in *this* life. Some promises can't be banked on this side of eternity, and that is the problem with most televangelists. They are teaching Word of Faith doctrines, which we will soon see are unbiblical and utterly false. I have seen firsthand the deception that goes on in the movement, and so I have found myself with a strong burden to expose the falsehoods therein and to help others learn how to discern those lies. I firmly believe that the Word of Faith movement (and the spread of its equally corrupt legacy) is responsible for the greatest amount of deception in the church today. Most believers know that when the Mormons or JW's come to the door, they are presenting a false gospel. However, they will shut that door, turn on the TV, and invite false teachers into their homes, allowing them to explain the Christian life to them, with no clue that they are being fed false hope and empty promises. Yes, there are some pastors on TV who teach biblically, but they are a definite and shrinking minority. As we will see, most televangelists promote Word of Faith, and we're about to see how that is an utterly false gospel.

The greatest source of frustration for myself and other Christians whose eyes have been opened is that it is incredibly difficult to make people understand that Word of Faith teachers are false teachers in the first place. The inevitable responses are predictable: *"But they love Jesus! They talk about being born again! They praise God! People come to Christ through them! They use scripture! They're so encouraging!"* And this is the conundrum that makes it so hard for people to understand what the problem is. Yes, they say all those things, *but what they are really saying is not what you think they are saying.* I know how confusing that sounds, but if you'll bear with me a bit further, you will see that the Jesus they speak of is *not* the Jesus of scripture. The born again experience they speak of does *not* mean the same thing as what scripture teaches about the new birth. The God they refer to bears little resemblance to the majestic, almighty, omnipotent and sovereign God of scripture. In fact, their God is more like a superhero or a genie in a bottle. Their God is limited, and not in control of His own creation. People come to Christ, but it is a *false, man-made* Christ they are embracing. The scriptures they quote are invariably taken out of context and misapplied. The encouragement they offer can surely brighten your day, but what are they encouraging you with? In many cases, they are cheering you up with false hopes and empty promises! Yes, those are serious allegations, but if you'll bear with me, you will see that these charges are absolutely true and are not a matter of my - or anyone else's opinions. They are a matter of public record, yet all of this goes over most people's heads.

Word of Faith can be hard to pin down as it is not a specific church or denomination, but rather a *belief system* that has its own unique doctrines and theology, which cannot be supported by any serious study of scripture. Only by cherry-picking verses out of context, (*also known as proof-texting*) and twisting the meaning can they claim any scriptural support. So, let's look at a primer on the Word of Faith movement to get an idea of what they believe and teach.

Word of Faith 101

In the beginning ... Word of Faith theology teaches that God lives on a physical planet called Heaven and created our world and mankind out of a desire to reproduce Himself. Therefore, since we are the product of God's reproduction, we ourselves are *little gods.* So, Adam was an exact copy of God, with no difference between them. Man was created to be the *god* of this world, just like God rules over planet Heaven. When man sinned in the Garden, he lost his dominion over the earth and gave legal rights to Satan. (There are a lot of cosmic laws and legalities in Word of Faith theology.) At the same time, God desperately wanted to intervene, but since He lost His legal right, His hands were tied. The only way God could intervene is by taking advantage of other spiritual laws, like the power of the spoken word. The power of words is crucial to Word of Faith theology. Since we are gods, our spoken words have creative power, and can even move the hand of God; even *give God permission to act.* Word of Faith adherents believe that God cannot do anything in our world unless one of us speaks it into existence, and thus enters into an agreement with God. Any serious student of The Word should know that God needs neither our permission nor our words to permit Him to act. He alone is God. We are not. Furthermore, they believe that faith is a *force* which can be manipulated by our spoken words. (This is why some authors have *(sarcastically)* referred to Word of Faith as *Star Wars Theology!*) They even that say God used the *faith-force* to speak creation into being. You will hear them say things like *God used His faith to create the universe,* or worse, *Have the faith of God!* Biblically speaking, faith is simply believing in God, it is not a *force* like in Star Wars! God is the *object* of faith. He doesn't need to *have* faith. I'm going to summarize a lot here, but it gets even more ridiculous.

God wanted to send Jesus to redeem mankind, but it took a long, long time as everything He wanted to do was held in limbo until He could get someone down here to speak His plans into being. God wanted to bring Jesus into the world but couldn't start the process until that magic day when Abraham spoke the conception of Isaac into being. *Note: you won't find this anywhere in scripture, but Word of Faith teachers would have us believe that they get a lot of their doctrine by divine revelation, something that should always be regarded with a high level of skepticism.* God had to wait for ages for Jesus to be born because it required a combination of His prophets speaking Jesus into existence and finding a suitable virgin whom he could get to speak the right words to allow Jesus to be conceived within her. It takes a long time to find a virgin willing to go for that whole immaculate conception thing. And it gets worse...

Word of Faith teachings about Jesus are so unbiblical and even blasphemous, I would hope that anyone whose eyes are opened to it, would never desire to listen to a Word of Faith teacher ever again, no matter how positive some of their other teachings may sound. Remember that one reason deception works are that it often comes tangled up in a significant amount of truth! All false teachers say *some* things that are true. They also quote scriptures *(usually out of context and misinterpreted)* to back up their statements.

When it comes to the nature and character of Jesus, not all WOF teachers are in total agreement, so I'll present the majority consensus. All of them teach something along the lines that Jesus was not fully divine in His incarnation, and / or that He was just a man in right relationship with God. This is interesting because the ones who claim an anointing to perform all manner of signs and wonders say that if Jesus could heal the sick and raise the dead as an ordinary man, so can we. Later on, we will examine how utterly unbiblical such claims are. Some WOF teachers claim that Jesus did not become the son of God until His baptism, a doctrine called *adoptionism.* Others claim He did not become the son of God until he was raised from the dead.

One of the most unbiblical WOF teachings is that the crucifixion was not enough to atone for our sins and that Jesus needed to be punished and tormented by demons in hell for three days, something found *nowhere* in scripture. Scripture tells us that right before Jesus died, He said, *"It is finished! Father into your hands I commit my spirit!"* The work of redemption was complete. Furthermore, when the thief hanging next to Him expressed belief, Jesus said, "*This day*, you will be with me in Paradise."

From here it gets even worse. Many WOF teachers say that Jesus actually *became a satanic being,* and therefore *had* to be punished in hell. Part of this unbiblical doctrine is that *Jesus died spiritually; that he died two deaths.* This can sound confusing, but according to many Word of Faith teachers, somewhere between Gethsemane and the cross, *Jesus took on the nature of Satan and became guilty of sin,* no different than any ordinary sinner. This is not just doctrinal confusion here; this is blasphemy! If Jesus took on the nature of Satan, He could not have been the sinless sacrifice God required for our redemption. According to scripture, Jesus bore the *punishment* for our sins, but He never became *guilty* of sin. There is an enormous difference.

Next, they claim that to be raised from the dead and truly become the son of God, Jesus had to become born again in hell, making him the first person to experience the new birth. No amount of tortuous scripture twisting can support these fantasies in any viable way. One thing to note is that the Hebrew word, *Sheol* which gets translated into English as *hell,* simply means *grave;* the abode of the dead. Scripture does note that Jesus descended into the abode of the dead to proclaim his victory over sin and death. But for Jesus to have been tormented in flames would mean that he was cast into the Lake of Fire, which scripture says will be unpopulated until the final judgment. The teaching that demons tormented Jesus on their own turf can be easily refuted by scriptures demonstrating that Satan and his minions will not be sent to hell until the final judgment. They are here on earth seeking to deceive us right now! Remember in the book of Job, how Satan reported to God about where he had been...

Job 1:6-7 Updated American Standard Version (UASV)

⁶ Now there was a day when the sons of God came to present themselves before Jehovah, and Satan also came among them. ⁷ Jehovah said to Satan, "From where do you come?" Then Satan answered Jehovah and said, "From roaming about on the earth and walking around on it."

Satan is not in hell.[16] *He dreads and fears the day when he will be! This scenario of demons having Jesus in their clutches, in their own domain is pure man-made fiction!*

> **1:6.** The scene suddenly shifts to heaven, providing a rare insight into the unseen world above. **One day the angels came to present**

---

[16] HERE ARE SOME BLOG ARTICLES THAT ARE BASED IN SCRIPTURE:
TINY URLs Hellfire – Eternal Torment? (http://tiny.cc/pmnwsy), What Did Jesus Teach About Hell? (http://tiny.cc/7hnwsy), Is Hellfire Part of Divine Justice? (http://tiny.cc/gnnwsy) Is the Hellfire Doctrine Truly Just? (http://tiny.cc/0nnwsy), The Bible's Viewpoint of Death (http://tiny.cc/9nnwsy) Do Humans Have a Soul that Is Apart From Us? (http://tiny.cc/4onwsy)

themselves before the LORD. This implies that this day was like any other day. The sons of God were the angelic hosts (Job 38:7; Gen. 6:2) who were reporting to the Lord by coming before the divine throne. These ministering spirits had been away, serving the Lord, and they returned for further orders. In the midst of this gathering, **Satan also came with them.** Once the highest archangel, Satan[17] had been banished from heaven for his rebellion against God. Yet, mysteriously, he still could approach God's throne in heaven. So Satan joined them, once again, on this occasion.

1:7. The LORD asked Satan, "Where have you come from?" The omniscient God knew where Satan had been, as well as what he had been doing. This question was intended to elicit a confession from this fallen angel. Satan answered the LORD, "From roaming through the earth and going back and forth in it." This was the devil's main activity, wreaking havoc on the earth as a "roaring lion looking for someone to devour" (1 Pet. 5:8). Never idle, Satan is always on the prowl as "the prince of this world" (John 12:31), blinding minds (2 Cor. 4:4), stealing God's Word (Matt. 13:19), opposing God's work (1 Thess. 2:18), sowing tares (Matt. 13:37–40), tempting God's people (1 Cor. 7:5), attacking God's Word (Gen. 3:1), spreading false doctrine (1 Tim. 1:3), persecuting God's church (Rev. 2:10), and deceiving the nations (Rev. 16:14).[18]

Now it must be noted that these teachings change the very nature and definition of what it means to be born again. Word of Faith teaches that

---

[17] **CHRISTIAN PUBLISHING HOUSE NOTE:** The Holman Old and New Testament Commentary volumes are among the most trusted commentaries that any Christian could study. However, they are not correct one hundred percent of the time because of human imperfection like anyone else. Everything said above is correct except for the claim that "the highest archangel, Satan." This is wrong on two fronts: First, there is only one archangel. Second, the Bible explicitly names this archangel, Michael. Third, nowhere in Scripture does it even infer that Satan is an archangel. See https://christianpublishinghouse.co/word-of-the-day/

Archangel: (Gr. *archangelos*) Michael is the only spirit named as an archangel in the Bible. Nevertheless, some Bible scholars believe that 'it is possible that there are other' archangels. However, the prefix "arch," meaning "chief" or "principal," indicates that there is only one archangel, the chief angel. Yes, Gabriel is very powerful, but no Scripture ever refers to him as an archangel. If there were multiple archangels, how could they even be described as an arch (chief or principal) angel? In the Scriptures, "archangel" is never found in the plural. Clearly, Michael is the only archangel and as the highest-ranking angel, like the highest-ranking general in the army, Michael stands directly under the authority of God, as he commands the other angels, including Gabriel, according to the Father's will and purposes. Michael, the Archangel, whose name means, "Who is like God?"); he disputed with Satan over Moses body. (Jude 9) Michael with Gabriel stood guard over the sons of Israel and fought for Israel against demons. (Dan. 10:13, 21) He cast Satan and the demons out of heaven. (Rev. 12:7-9) He will defeat the kings of the earth and their armies at Armageddon, and he will be the one given the privilege of abyssing Satan, the archenemy of God. – Rev. 18:1-2; 19:11-21.

[18] Anders, Max. Holman Old Testament Commentary Volume 10 - Job (Kindle Locations 618-631). B&H Publishing. Kindle Edition.

since Jesus became divine by the new birth when we are born again we become every bit as much a *son of God*, every bit as much an incarnation of God as Jesus Christ. Think for a moment how blasphemous and unbiblical these teachings are, diminishing the glory of Christ and elevating mankind to the status of gods! Many Word of Faith teachers even denies that Jesus was the *only* begotten Son of God, a clear contradiction of John 3:16, claiming that we also become begotten sons of God when we experience the new birth. The sad thing is that most people who listen to WOF teachers every day are unaware of these teachings. That's because most WOF teachers choose to whitewash or bury these notions in a sea of ambiguity. Some, like Kenneth Copeland, are extremely blatant about it while others are much subtler. In general, their tactic is to preach a lot uplifting and encouraging things *(appealing to itching ears, just as scripture warns!)* to draw people in. Then, once people are impressed and grow fond of these teachers, they start wanting to check out their books and CD's, and that's where they start to consume outright heresy. The enemy is subtle and crafty indeed.

Understanding WOF teachings on God, Jesus and the meaning of being born again are crucial to understanding what they teach regarding man, and what the Christian life is all about. Since we are sons of God and indeed *little gods*, our spoken words have supernatural power to make things happen - thus the term, *Word of Faith.* Therefore, they teach that we can *name and claim* all the things we desire from God such as health, prosperity, and material comforts. And because we are just as much incarnations of God as Jesus, we can assume we have the power to heal the sick, raise the dead and prophesy just like Jesus and the Apostles did. They justify these teachings by cherry picking scriptures out of context and twisting their meaning. They will often appeal to scriptures like Isaiah 53:5 - *By His stripes we are healed*, to claim that physical healing was purchased in the atonement, and can be claimed just like salvation, by faith. They don't like to hear that the Hebrew word translated as *healed*, more accurately refers to *being made whole spiritually*. There is no scriptural promise of perfect health for every believer this side of heaven, something we'll explore in depth later. Similarly, they'll quote, *I pray that you prosper*, from 3 John 2 to claim that God wants all believers to be wealthy. They don't like to address the fact that the verse they are quoting is simply a standard greeting in a first-century letter, the equivalent of us writing to someone and saying, *"How are you? I hope you're doing well."* They don't want to acknowledge that the Greek word translated as *prosper*, simply means to have things go well for you; to have your needs met. Most of the intended readership of the New Testament were dirt poor and would be considered prosperous if they had the necessities of life, like food, water, and clothing. So far, we've just looked at a bare bone outline of WOF teachings. It goes much deeper than what we've discussed here and had also spawned other unbiblical movements like the New Apostolic Reformation, which we will explore in another section.

Going forward we'll unpack the origins of these teachings, who popularized them, and who is promoting them today. The names may be surprising and familiar. Before you take offense at seeing some of your favorite teachers mentioned, ask yourself if your loyalty is to God or to certain popular teachers. If I mention anyone, I will demonstrate by their own words, compared to scripture that they are teaching unbiblical doctrines. It is not my intent to engage in character assassination, but the truth must be told. As for the individuals teaching these things, I'm sure some of them are very sincere; they may truly believe what they teach. Others may be deliberate cons, telling people what they want to hear to enrich themselves. Not knowing their hearts, I cannot say with certainty where various teachers fall on this continuum, but we will demonstrate from their own teachings, and by comparing them with scripture that they are indisputably false teachers. One thing to keep in mind as we explore WOF teachers in greater depth is that in their own way, they mimic the very first temptation Satan offered mankind in the Garden; "*Hath God said?*"

Genesis 3:1-5 Updated American Standard Version (UASV)

3 Now the serpent was more crafty than any beast of the field which Jehovah God had made. And he said to the woman, "Did God actually say, 'You[19] shall not eat of any tree in the garden'?" **2** And the woman said to the serpent, "From the fruit of the trees of the garden we may eat, **3** but from the tree that is in the midst of the garden, God said, 'You shall not eat from it, nor shall you touch it, lest you die.'" **4** And the serpent said to the woman, "You shall not surely die. **5** For God knows that when you eat of it your eyes will be opened, and you will be like God, knowing good and evil." knowing good and evil.

Part of Satan's initial ploy was to question the words of God and offer man a chance to be elevated to God-like status. The Word of Faith movement does the very same thing.

> Later Bible texts establish Satan the Devil as the one using a serpent as his mouthpiece like a ventriloquist would a dummy. Anyway, take note that Satan contradicts the clear statement that God made to Adam at Genesis 2:17, "you will not surely die." Backing up a little, we see Satan asking an inferential question, "Did God actually say, 'You shall not eat of any tree in the garden'?" First, he is overstating what he knows

---

[19] In Hebrew *you* is plural in verses 1–5

to be true, not "any tree," just one tree. Second, Satan is inferring, 'I can't believe that God would say . . . how dare he say such.' Notice too that Eve has been told so thoroughly about the tree that she even goes beyond what Adam told her, not just that you 'do not eat from it,' no, 'you do not even touch it!' Then, Satan out and out lied and slandered God as a liar, saying that 'they would not die.' To make matters much worse, he infers that God is withholding good from them, and by rebelling they would be better off, being like God, 'knowing good and bad.' This latter point is not knowledge of; it is the self-sovereignty of choosing good and bad for oneself and act of rebellion for created creatures. What was symbolized by the tree is well expressed in a footnote on Genesis 2:17, in The Jerusalem Bible (1966):

This knowledge is a privilege which God reserves to himself and which man, by sinning, is to lay hands on, 3:5, 22. Hence it does not mean omniscience, which fallen man does not possess; nor is it moral discrimination, for unfallen man already had it and God could not refuse it to a rational being. It is the power of deciding for himself what is good and what is evil and of acting accordingly, a claim to complete moral independence by which man refuses to recognize his status as a created being. The first sin was an attack on God's sovereignty, a sin of pride.

The Issues at Hand

(1) Satan called God a liar and said he was not to be trusted, as to the life or death issue.

(2) Satan's challenge, therefore, took into question the right and legitimacy of God's rightful place as the Universal Sovereign.

(3) Satan also suggested that people would remain obedient to God only as long as their submitting to God was to their benefit.

(4) Satan all but said that humankind was able to walk on his own, there being no need for dependence on God.

(5) Satan argued that man could be like God, choosing for himself what is right and wrong.

(6) Satan claimed that God's way of ruling was not in the best interests of humans, and they could do better without God.[20]

Origins of the Word of Faith Movement

An in-depth history of Word of Faith could go way, way back but to provide a basic understanding, we will look at one of the first men to popularize this belief system, Pentecostal preacher Kenneth Hagin (1917-

---

[20] Why has God Permitted Wickedness and Suffering?
https://christianpublishinghouse.co/2016/10/05/why-has-god-permitted-wickedness-and-suffering/

2003). Hagin started his ministry in the early 1930's with many dubious claims of personal revelations from Jesus, Himself. Keep in mind that revelations from the Author of scripture will never result in teachings *(and an entire belief system)* that contradict His Word on multiple levels. Hagin was intrigued by a man named E.W. Kenyon, who sought to incorporate mystical and New Age ideas into Christianity, chiefly the idea that our thoughts and words have the power to create our desired reality. So intrigued was Hagin with Kenyon, that he outright plagiarized the man for his own books. Virtually all the unbiblical teachings we've looked at so far can be found in Hagin's writings. The idea that we are gods, that our spoken words have power to create, the flat-out heresy that Jesus, in His incarnation was not divine, and had to be born again in hell - they all are present in Hagin's writings and teachings.

Sadly, his heretical teachings only scratch the surface of his bizarre legacy. His meetings were known for many strange manifestations, which he attributed to the Holy Spirit; things like people levitating in his services or being stuck to the floor with *Holy Ghost glue,* or standing in trance-like statues, for days on end. He was also an early advocate of such anomalies as being *drunk in the spirit.* There is a video easily found on Google or YouTube, (simply type *Kenneth Hagin drunk in the spirit*) of a Hagin service where he indeed appears so intoxicated that some assistants must support him as he staggers around the venue, imparting this drunkenness to others. With a wave of his hand entire rows of people falls out of their chairs laughing hysterically. In one scene, he approaches a keyboard player on the stage and waves his hand at him. The musician briefly looks like he's about to break down in tears, and then suddenly he's jumping and dancing and running around the stage as if he's being stricken by fire ants. Soon the whole congregation is acting in like manner. I'll concede that some of us are more emotional than others, and there is nothing wrong with emotionally expressive worship, in and of itself. And it must be noted that there are Pentecostals and charismatics who seek to worship biblically, despite perhaps having divergent views from mainline Protestants on things like tongues, healing, and prophecy. *(Some - not all - more conservative Christians hold to a belief that the "sign gifts" of healing, tongues, and prophecy ceased with the completion of the written scriptures; charismatics tend to believe they are still in operation. We will discuss this in greater detail in another section.)* Sadly, an overwhelming majority of modern charismatics have totally bought into WOF doctrines, as well as all manner of bizarre manifestations attributed to the Holy Spirit. The best way I can describe what I saw in that video was a circus-like atmosphere of chaos and confusion. Scripture tells us that things in the church are to be done in an orderly manner and that God is not the author of confusion. Not to mention that one of the fruits of the spirit is self-control...

Galatians 5:22-23 Updated American Standard Version (UASV)

[22] But the fruit of the Spirit is love, joy, peace, patience, kindness, goodness, faithfulness, [23] gentleness, self-control; against such things there is no law.

Falling down, and rolling on the floor like drunks hardly reflects self-control, does it? There is no way I can conclude that Hagin's teachings and practices were biblical.

> **5:22–23.** In contrast to the "acts of the flesh" presented above, those who are obedient to the Holy Spirit produce beautiful, nourishing spiritual fruit. Notice the fruit in this passage is called the fruit of the Spirit, not the fruit of self-effort. This fruit the Holy Spirit produces in the life of a faithful Christian. In other passages of Scripture, we are commanded to fulfill the individual characteristics. The answer to this seeming paradox, I believe, is that only the Holy Spirit can produce the fruit; but he will not do so unless we are striving to the best of our ability for them in faithful obedience. These fruits of the Spirit are in harmony with and not opposed to the law. However, they are not produced by the law but rather by the Spirit working through the believer's faith.[21]

The Dake Reference Bible

No discussion of the Word of Faith movement would be complete without looking at the Dake Reference Bible. Finnis Dake (1902-1987) was a Pentecostal preacher, who compiled a study Bible with notes and commentaries that have profoundly influenced the Pentecostal and Charismatic movements. In his notes can be found a litany of errors that most WOF teachers still promote to this day. Among them are: false teaching on the Trinity; he taught *three separate gods,* rather than *One God in three persons*, he denied that God is omniscient, omnipresent, and omnipotent - even making a statement that God learns about events in real time, just like we do, he also wrote that God has a physical body with both male and female parts, that God eats meals, sleeps, and travels from place to place. One of his strangest teachings was that each "god" in the Trinity has their own body, soul, and spirit; therefore, there are nine of them! As we look at individual Word of Faith teachers going forward, keep in mind that Dake's heretical doctrines have been embraced and promoted by some

---

[21] Max Anders, *Galatians-Colossians,* vol. 8, Holman New Testament Commentary (Nashville, TN: Broadman & Holman Publishers, 1999), 65.

of today's most prominent speakers, such as Benny Hinn, Kenneth Copeland, Joyce Meyer and scores of others. That should speak volumes.

"I thank God for the people who produced the Dake Bible. Their hard work has made it easier for me to teach God's Word."

• *Joyce Meyer (Word of Faith teacher)*

"The Dake Bible helped me build a solid foundation in the Word."

• *Creflo Dollar (Word of Faith Teacher)*

"The Dake Bible is one of the greatest literary works ever made for Pentecostal and Charismatic believers."

• *Rod Parsley (Word of Faith Teacher)*

CHAPTER 2 Kenneth Copeland

Having looked at Hagin, whom many consider the spiritual father of modern-day Word of Faith, we'll move on to his disciples, and take a closer look at them, as they are the ones propagating these falsehoods today. Again, Word of Faith is neither a church nor a denomination, but a belief system, and if that belief system were to have a de facto figurehead, one would need to look no further than Kenneth Copeland. Copeland is one of the most successful televangelists operating today, with an estimated net worth of over $700 million dollars. With an extravagant mansion, private jets, and a worldwide media empire, Copeland is a perfect example of why *Word of Faith, Health and Wealth Gospel, and Prosperity Gospel* are all synonyms for the same thing. Copeland teaches that God always desires for his people to be wealthy and to walk in divine, perfect health. It is no surprise that Copeland learned much of his theology from Hagin and Dake. While many modern WOF teachers like to disguise the belief system's more controversial tenets, Copeland holds his heresies aloft like a proud banner.

As with Hagin, Copeland openly teaches that we are gods. In one of his more famous statements on the matter, he says, *"You don't just have a god in you. You are one!"* In another example, Copeland is on record as saying,

"I say this with all respect so that it don't upset you too bad, but I say it anyway. When I read in the Bible where He (Jesus) says, 'I Am,' I just smile and say, 'Yes, I Am, too!"

And of course, if we are gods, it naturally follows that our spoken words have the power to bring things into existence. Today, most if not all WOF teachers credit Copeland with shaping their theology. Kenneth Copeland Ministries is responsible for all manner of nonsense being propagated today. For example, his wife Gloria claims that Christians have the power to control the weather and to rebuke storms just as Jesus did. *(We know Jesus could do that because He is God; we're not!)* Not surprisingly, the Copelands have been missing in action when various hurricanes and tornadoes have wreaked havoc upon the earth, making their claims of weather control rather dubious at best. And in one of the most disturbing statements I've heard him make on his TV program, Believer's Voice of Victory, he said that because speaking things into existence employs universal spiritual laws, even witches get results from it! So here he is, advocating the same thing witches do for believers! Some critics have called Word of Faith nothing more than Christian spell-casting and incantations! Let that sink in for a

Minute....

One reason people like Copeland seem to be okay with incorporating occult and New Age practices into Christianity is the notion that the occultists and New Agers stole their techniques from God's people, and therefore, why can't we reclaim them? You'll also find this line of reasoning with the New Apostolic Reformation, which we'll discuss later on. But let's look at what scripture has to say about such practices? Clearly, God is not okay with such things...

Leviticus 20:27 Updated American Standard Version (UASV)

[27] 'Now a man or a woman who is spirit medium or a spiritist[22] shall surely be put to death. They shall be stoned with stones, their bloodguiltiness is upon them.'"

It should be clear that Scripture forbids occult practices!

Deuteronomy 18:10-12 Updated American Standard Version (UASV)

[10] There shall not be found among you anyone who makes his son or his daughter pass through the fire, one who uses divination, one who practices witchcraft, or one who interprets omens, or a sorcerer, [11] or one who casts a spell, or a medium, or a spiritist, or one who calls up the dead. [12] For whoever does these things is detestable to Jehovah; and because of these detestable things Jehovah your God will drive them out before you.

18:10-11. The general principle is translated into specific prohibitions. Israel was not to imitate the practice of child sacrifice in an effort to appease a pagan deity and influence the course of the future. They were not to practice divination, the consulting of objects or people (living or dead) to discover what would happen in the future (see "Deeper Discoveries").

Israel was also prohibited from engaging in **sorcery**, the art of the occult. Sorcerers were, according to the literal meaning of the Hebrew text, "those who cause to appear." Their apparitions could seduce Israel into abandoning the worship of Yahweh. The Old Testament recognizes the reality of the spirit world and does not prohibit Israel from dabbling in it because of its ineffectiveness but because of its association with pagan deities.

Nor could the people of God tolerate the presence among them of one who interpreted **omens**, predicting the future on the basis of how objects fell out of a cup (cp. Gen. 44:5), for example.

---

[22] A person supposed to be able to foresee the future: seer, oracle, fortune-teller.

Witchcraft was also excluded as a method of discovering future events. The category includes those who performed what were (or appeared to be) supernaturally caused signs. Often these were designed to expel evil (Isa. 47:9,12).

The person who casts **spells** was thought to be able to use curses to control the destiny of others. The **medium** was one who practiced necromancy (as did the **spiritist**), attempting to contact **the dead** to obtain special information. Sometimes special vocal sounds were used to invoke these spirits (Isa. 8:19; cp. Lev. 20:6,27; 1 Sam. 28:3,9; 2 Kgs. 21:6).

18:12-14. Such detestable practices as those Moses cataloged had led God to drive out those nations who were in the land. Israel would risk a similar expulsion if they should take part in such exercises. Nor could such black arts be pursued as a sideline by only a few people in Israel. Anyone who engaged in these practices was detestable to the LORD. Israel was to be upright or blameless and to abhor such practices.

DEEPER DISCOVERIES

B. Divination (18:10)

Divination was the practice of determining the future by means of occult practices. These included oneiromancy (the interpretation of dreams), astrology, necromancy, augury (the analysis of the movements of birds and animals), pyromancy (the observation of patterns in fire), and especially haruspicy, the study of the entrails—especially the liver—of specified animals. Some of these methods are described in Ezekiel 21:21: "For the king of Babylon will stop at the fork in the road, at the junction of the two roads, to seek an omen: He will cast lots with arrows, he will consult his idols, he will examine the liver."

Joseph, unrecognized by his brothers, said to them, "What is this you have done? Don't you know that a man like me can find things out by divination?" (Gen 44:15). Benjamin had been arrested for having a divining cup in his grain sack, and Joseph was playing his role of pagan Egyptian viceroy to the hilt, so it is probable that his statement should not be taken as a description of what he actually did. However, it certainly can be regarded as typical of what Egyptian officials were expected to do at that time. All forms of divination and magic are off limits for God's people.[23]

Anyone still think that God is okay with occult practices?

---

[23] Anders, Max. Holman Old Testament Commentary - Deuteronomy: 3 (pp. 223-224, 227-228). B&H Publishing. Kindle Edition.

Copeland's next major heresy is his teaching that *God was the biggest failure in the whole bible!* Yes, he actually said that explaining that at the very beginning, God lost his most beautiful angel (the fall of Satan), he lost his most prized creation - the god-man Adam, and he lost dominion over the earth. These blasphemies are central to virtually all WOF teachings. Because man's fall gave Satan the legal right to dominion over the earth, God was now on the outside looking in, legally forbidden from intervening; no longer sovereign. I'd like to hear Copeland try to explain away Psalms 115:3 as well as so many other scriptures that testify to the sovereignty of God...

Psalm 115:3 Updated American Standard Version (UASV)

³ But our God is in the heavens;
he does all that he pleases.

Does this verse imply that God is in any way limited in His ability to accomplish His will? Absolutely not!

> **115:3**. The psalmist answered this Gentile sneer, saying God is alive in **heaven** and rules over all from his throne. Enthroned above, there is no diminishing of God's sovereignty, even in the presence of many trials. God does **whatever pleases him**, meaning his sovereignty is unequaled, unrivaled, and unopposed (Ps. 103:19). Even if Israel is defeated, it is God's doing, not his failure. When victory comes to Israel, this, too, is God's doing. No so-called god or idol-worshipping nation can oppose him.[24]

As noted in the introduction, God's plan to send Jesus for our redemption couldn't unfold until He could persuade Abraham to say the right words, by which he spoke Isaac, the forerunner of the messianic line into being.

A third tenet of Copeland's theology is that Jesus never claimed to be God; that He performed miracles of healings and resurrections as just an ordinary man in right relationship with God and empowered by the Holy Spirit. I would hope that any believer with even a cursory knowledge of scripture could refute this idea in a matter of seconds. Does Scripture not say the opposite...?

John 10:30 Updated American Standard Version (UASV)

³⁰ I and the Father are one."

---

[24] Lawson, Steven. Holman Old Testament Commentary - Psalms 76-150 (Kindle Locations 5456-5461). B&H Publishing Group. Kindle Edition.

What can this verse mean other than that Jesus Christ and God the Father are one and the same? Some commentaries indicate that the Greek word translated as "one" means of one essence.

Christian Publishing House would disagree with the author here when it comes to John 10:30. Regarding John 10:30, John Calvin (who was a Trinitarian) rightly said, "The ancients made a wrong use of this passage to prove that Christ is (ὁμοούσιος) of the same essence with the Father. For Christ does not argue about the unity of substance, but about the agreement which he has with the Father, so that whatever is done by Christ will be confirmed by the power of his Father."[25] This is not to say that CPH disagrees with the Trinity doctrine but rather that this verse can be used to support the said doctrine.

John 14:8-9 Updated American Standard Version (UASV)

8 Philip said to him, "Lord, show us the Father, and it is enough for us." 9 Jesus said to him, "Have I been so long with you, and yet you have not come to know me, Philip? He who has seen me has seen the Father; how can you say, 'Show us the Father'?

Again, Jesus makes it quite clear that He and the Father are One.

Again, **Christian Publishing House** would disagree with the author. Jesus stated many times that all that he did was according to the will of the Father not his own will, meaning that any who overserved what he was doing was, in essence, overserving the Father. In his notes on John 14:9, Bible commentator Albert Barnes states: *"Hath seen the Father.* This cannot refer to the *essence* or *substance* of God, for he is invisible, and in that respect no man has seen God at any time. All that is meant when it is said that *God is seen,* is, that some *manifestation* of Him has been made; or some such *exhibition* as that we may learn his *character,* his *will,* and his *plans....* The knowledge of the Son was itself, of course, the knowledge of the Father. There was such an intimate *union* in their nature and design, that he who understood the one did also the other."[26] Again, this is not to say that CPH disagrees with the Trinity doctrine but rather that this verse can be used to support the said doctrine.

Other scriptures confirm that in his incarnation, Jesus was both fully God and fully man, something theologians call the *hypostasis union.* Copeland claims that Jesus Himself appeared to him and revealed that He never claimed to be God! How sad that people would believe Copeland's

---

[25] John Calvin and William Pringle, *Commentary on the Gospel according to John,* vol. 1 (Bellingham, WA: Logos Bible Software, 2010), 417.

[26] Albert Barnes, *Notes on the New Testament: Explanatory and Practical. Vol. X: James, Peter, John, and Jude* (London, England: Thomas Nelson, 1847), 423.

alleged revelations over the very scriptures they contradict! It is clear to see how this theology diminishes the glory of Christ and elevates man to the status of a god - pure blasphemy!

A fourth problematic tenet of Copeland's theology is his parroting of Hagin's doctrine that Jesus had to atone for our sins in hell and be born again as if the cross were insufficient. Copeland takes this doctrine to an even more blasphemous level by asserting that if dying on a cross were enough to atone for man's sins, *anyone* could have done it. Copeland even has the gall to say that had he been alive in 33 AD, *he* could have died for our sins! Do I even have to say how blasphemous this is? So again, with the cross being insufficient, Jesus had to pay for our sins in hell and become the first born-again man. I challenge anyone to search the scriptures and find one morsel of support for this doctrine. You won't - since once again, Copeland expects us to believe that these teachings are the product of direct revelation from Christ, Himself. We will also see that Copeland's army of clones and disciples are out there promoting these notions, and it is baffling that Christians who should know better, believe these alleged revelations simply because Copeland, and his army of devotees quote some twisted scriptures - *out of context, of course* - and couch their sermons with enough Christian-sounding lingo to appear biblical. Let's think back to when Paul commended the Bereans for diligently searching the scriptures night and day to see if his teachings were so. We are living in a day where many are being deceived simply because they are placing too much trust in their favorite teachers, without searching the scriptures to see if those teachings are true.

JOYCE MEYER

I know I'll be offending some readers, as Joyce Meyer is an extremely popular teacher, and people tend to find her messages uplifting. But bear with me, and we will see that Meyer is definitely a proud Word of Faith teacher, although her approach is usually so smooth that people can listen to her for years, even decades, and allow her aberrant theology to slip right under the radar. She has an enormous talent for making scripture appear to say that which it does not. I will concede that many of her messages sound positive, but when we examine the core doctrines upon which her teachings are based, you will have to decide if she is someone that you should be listening to. Joyce Meyer attended Rhema College, a school founded by none other than Kenneth Hagin. That should be a huge red flag right there. Also take note that Meyer considers Hagin her spiritual father, even referring to him at times as, *"Dad Hagin."*

And although she doesn't say it as often, or as clearly as Copeland, Meyer is clearly on record as teaching that we are little gods, that Jesus needed to be born again in hell, and that our words have the power to create our reality. Despite her frequent ambiguity, a simple internet search will lead you to numerous video and audio examples of Joyce teaching these very things. You will also find quotes from her books, where she puts these things on the printed page for all to see. One thing she is very well known for is saying, *"Call those things that be not as though they are..."* to encourage her listeners to speak their desires into existence. This is an abhorrent abuse of Romans 4: 17, so let's look at the verse. Once again, context does matter...

Romans 4:17 Updated American Standard Version (UASV)

[17] (as it is written, "A father of many nations have I made you") in the presence of Him whom he believed, even God, who gives life to the dead and who calls the things that are not as though they are,

This passage is referring to Abraham and his faith in God, the only one who can speak things into being. Nothing in the passage implies that we can do the same. No amount of tortuous scripture twisting can wrench such a meaning out of the verse, yet millions of people believe it means that, just because Joyce Meyer says so. Of course, if one accepts the belief that we are gods, it's not that big a stretch to think that our words have supernatural and creative power.

> **4:16–17.** Paul's answer is the overall theme of the Bible: the promise will be fulfilled by grace through faith (Eph. 2:8–9). In fact, the only way that God could guarantee that Abraham and his descendants would become a great nation, that Abraham's name would be great in the earth, that he would be a blessing, that those who bless him and his descendants would qualify to be blessed, and that all the peoples on earth would be blessed by God (Gen. 12:1–3) was for God, by his grace, to promise that it would happen! **Therefore, the promise comes by faith, so that it may be by grace and may be guaranteed to all Abraham's offspring**—both to those who are Abraham's physical descendants and believe and to those who are his descendants by faith.
>
> Just as the Jews might have held to "Abraham said it, I believe it, and that settles it," Paul is now saying that "God promised it, Abraham believed it, and that settles it." As God continues to forgive, by his grace, the failures of Abraham and his descendants, the promise remains in effect. Should God "change his mind" (which he will not; Num. 23:19; 1 Sam. 15:29) and switch from grace to law, the "promise" would be annulled. When God told Abraham that he had made him "a father of many nations" (Gen. 17:5), that was a guarantee that the promise was a promise to be fulfilled by grace through faith.
>
> What kind of faith did it take for Abraham to hear that promise from God and believe, at his and Sarah's age, that **nations** would one

> day come from his loins? He had to believe that God was one who **gives life to the dead and calls things that are not as though they were**. In that way, Abraham foreshadowed the New Testament definition of faith: "being sure of what we hope for and certain of what we do not see" (Heb. 11:1). Abraham had to be "fully persuaded" (Rom. 4:21).
>
> Paul makes reference here to the deadness of Abraham's and Sarah's reproductive abilities. The God who gives life to dead things and calls into existence that which is not was the God who was speaking to Abraham. The God who, *ex nihilo* (out of nothing), created the heavens and the earth by speaking them into existence was the God who was speaking to Abraham. It is one thing to hear the accounts of creation as they were passed along by Noah and his sons after the flood, and to be amazed at what creation must have been like. But now Abraham was being challenged to let God do his creative work in him and his wife. This was different!
>
> All his life, Abraham had hoped for a son, and he finally reached a point where he was sure it would not happen. He had never seen his own progeny, and was probably certain that he would never see it. But now, he was being asked to hope again and to see for the first time. He was being asked to believe God.[27]

Once again, this a case where being a Berean would clear up a lot of confusion. I

once heard another WOF teacher, Andrew Wommack, teaching the same thing, and then going on to say that Isaac was conceived because Abraham's faith-filled words spoke him into existence. You will have an impossible task supporting this with scripture, yet most WOF teachers repeat this falsehood as if it were common knowledge.

Joyce's insistence that Jesus was born again in hell is also a matter of public record, although she has removed the teaching from more recent editions of the book in which she first said it, *The Most Important Decision You'll Ever Make*.

His spirit went to hell because that is where we deserve to go... There is no hope of anyone going to heaven unless they believe this truth."

(The Most Important Decision You'll Ever Make, by Joyce Meyer, second printing, May 1993, page 37)

Despite having removed the teaching, she has never renounced the doctrine or said she was wrong, so one can reasonably assume she's just

---

[27] Kenneth Boa and William Kruidenier, *Romans*, vol. 6, Holman New Testament Commentary (Nashville, TN: Broadman & Holman Publishers, 2000), 135–136.

trying to obfuscate this ever so controversial teaching. And you can see that she's taken it a step further, by stating that unless you believe with all your heart that Jesus took your place in hell, there is no hope of you going to heaven.

Where in scripture are we told that our salvation is contingent upon such an unbiblical belief? Nothing in the above quote is taught, or even implied in scripture. Like Copeland, Meyer expects us to believe that she got this via *revelation knowledge.* Later, we'll explore why anyone's claims of extra-biblical revelation should be regarded with extreme caution and held up to the light of what has already been revealed in scripture.

Her belief that we are little gods hangs on some almost comically flawed logic. She is on record as saying that if cows reproduce cattle kind, and so forth, what happens when God reproduces? He creates little gods!

"I was listening to a set of tapes by one man and he explained it like this..this kind of gets the point across...he said why do people have such a fit about God calling his creation, his creation, his man not his whole creation, but his man, little gods? If he's God what's he going to call them but the God kind? I mean if you as a human being have a baby you call it a human kind. If if [sic] cattle has another cattle they call it cattle kind. I mean what is God supposed to call 'em? Doesn't the Bible say we are created in his image? Now you understand I am not saying you are god with a capital G. That is not the issue here so don't go trying to stone me or yell blasphemy at me." "The Bible says right here, John 10: 34...'and Jesus answered is it not written in your law I say we are gods.' So, men are called Gods by the law..."(Joyce Meyer)

First, nothing in scripture should lead us to believe that we were created out of God's desire to reproduce Himself. God did not reproduce; He *created* us in His image. Being created in His image does not mean that we are gods, and no scriptures support this idea. *In His image* means that we were given certain characteristics that He shares with us, such as intellect, emotion, creativity, etc. The idea that we are little gods is pure WOF fantasy, an idea hatched from the vain imaginations of men.

As for her quoting Jesus, that men were called gods in Psalms 82:6, He was referring to the fact that the Old Testament judges were appointed to act as *lords and rulers* over the people, not that they were actually gods. He also went on to say they would die as men.

Another of Joyce's claims is that she is no longer a sinner. This is an obvious contradiction of scripture:

1 John 1:8 Updated American Standard Version (UASV)

[8] If we say we have no sin, we deceive ourselves, and the truth is not in us.

This verse requires very little explanation. None of us are without sin, no, not one!

> **1:8.** We do not know if the false teachers were suggesting that the Ephesian believers were without sin, or if that is an error the Ephesian believers fell into by themselves. Either way, it needs to be corrected. A person might not be conscious of sin, but this does not mean he or she is free from it.
>
> There are two kinds of sin—doing those things we ought not to do and not doing those things we should do. The longer we walk with Christ, the more likely it is that we will put aside more and more of the things we ought not to do. If we came to Christ as adults, we might be successful in putting away many of the overt sins we committed during our non-Christian days. We might no longer smoke and get drunk and curse and treat others abusively. We might go through a day or more in which we are not aware of committing an obvious sin.
>
> On the other hand, when we grasp that we are to do all the things that Jesus would do if he were in our shoes, we fail continually. None of us loves perfectly as Jesus did. Therefore, we sin, because a failure to love perfectly is a sin. If we think we are without sin altogether, we are deceived and we live a lie.[28]

When we become born again, our sins are forgiven, and we should certainly strive towards righteous living, but we will never be perfect this side of Heaven. Even the Apostle Paul admitted to struggling with sin. Meyer says that when she finally got it through her head that she's no longer a sinner, she stopped sinning. Well, right there she told a lie, so she's rather deluded, regardless of how sincere she is.

"I am not poor. I am not miserable, and I am not a sinner. That is a lie from the pit of hell. That is what I were and if I still was then Jesus died in vain. I'm going to tell you something folks. I didn't stop sinning until I finally got it through my thick head I wasn't a sinner anymore." - Joyce Meyer

If Joyce Meyer promoted herself as a motivational speaker, I might not be so critical. When it comes to matters of daily life, she often gives good practical advice, and sometimes even valid scriptural insights. But even a broken clock is right twice a day! The enemy is a master at delivering lies wrapped in a cloak of truth! Should we try to sift the good teachings out of her messages, while thinking we can avoid the heresy? The problem with trying to sift out the good is that people who have been listening to

---

[28] David Walls and Max Anders, *I & II Peter, I, II & III John, Jude*, vol. 11, Holman New Testament Commentary (Nashville, TN: Broadman & Holman Publishers, 1999), 157–158.

her for years remain oblivious to the fact that she's teaching Word of Faith doctrines in the first place! If you can't discern that much, how can you trust yourself to practice discernment regarding *anything* she says? Like scripture (The Apostle Paul) said...

Galatians 5:9 Updated American Standard Version (UASV)

⁹ A little leaven leavens the whole lump.

A valid interpretation would be that a little bit of heresy corrupts the entire message.

> **5:7–10.** The fourth negative consequence of returning to the law is that it hinders spiritual growth and development. Using the metaphor of a **race**, Paul states that the legalists had cut in on the Galatians' spiritual race and caused them to stumble spiritually. As a result, the Galatians were no longer **obeying the truth**. Turning to a yeast metaphor, Paul illustrates how quickly a little bit of legalism can contaminate a believer and, indeed, a whole church. Paul, however, expressed his confidence that the Galatians would not depart from the truth. He warned that those who are confusing them will experience God's judgment.[29]

JOEL OSTEEN

Stepping on toes yet again, we must look at the massively popular Joel Osteen, as he - like Meyer - is one of the most popular televangelists operating today. Like Meyer, his popularity stems largely from the uplifting and encouraging tone of his messages. Many people would reasonably ask what is wrong with that, but with Osteen, much of the problem is in what he does *not* say. He has never come right out and said that Jesus is the only way to salvation, waffling in interviews on questions about the eternal destiny of those who reject Christ. He also leaves a huge and vital chunk of the gospel message out of his sermons, by refusing to mention anything about sin, or the need for repentance to accompany belief.

While it is somewhat hard to pin him down doctrinally, he is a staunch advocate of *positive confessions*, which is just a verbal variant on calling those things that are not as though they were. Like Meyer, he tells us that scripture instructs us to "call those things that be not as though they are." Once again, it is truly baffling how virtually all Word of Faith teachers assign this application to Romans 4:17. As we've seen, the verse merely describes God as the One who can do that. There is not even the slightest hint of us being able to do the same! Yet, Osteen most certainly teaches that our

---

[29] Max Anders, *Galatians-Colossians*, vol. 8, Holman New Testament Commentary (Nashville, TN: Broadman & Holman Publishers, 1999), 63.

words have the power to create our destiny and make things happen; his books and messages are full of that belief. In one of his most popular books, *The Power of I Am*, he asserts that whatever we say after, "*I am,*" is what will happen to us. *(This is also known in the occult world as the Law of Attraction; you attract what you think and say. This is totally unbiblical. Did Jesus attract scourging and crucifixion? Did Job attract his misfortunes?)* This kind of teaching has more to do with the New Age and occultism than with inspired scripture, yet so many people wholeheartedly believe it. In fact, many of his teachings sound like they were taken from author Rhonda Byrne's *The Secret*, a popular New Age book, that puts forth that our thoughts create our reality. Substitute words for thoughts, and you have Word of Faith doctrine as presented by Osteen. Some have referred to his teachings as *Prosperity Lite,* but that in no way diminishes the fact that his messages state that God's will for us is always health, wealth, and comfort. He generally does not employ a Bible for any part of his sermons, other than to hold it up like a prop, and imply that he's about to teach from it; *"Say it like you mean it...Today I will be taught the Word of God..."* Actually, no - you won't.

While I don't deny that God *can* bless anyone he chooses with health and material things - *if and only if* - He sees fit, there are absolutely no guarantees in scripture that it is always His will to do so. Theologically, Osteen's lack of pastoral and biblical education is painfully obvious. Again, in various interviews, he has responded to questions about who will be saved - *and how* - plus questions regarding sin, with a repeated mantra of, *"I don't know..."* If he had studied scripture and knew it's doctrines, he would know. On matters of sin, he has dodged those questions by simply saying that he just doesn't *go there*. Any real preacher of the gospel would *go there*.

Like Meyer, he could possibly get a pass as a motivational speaker, but he most certainly does not preach the biblical gospel. There's no need to rehash every WOF doctrine for every teacher we examine as they all generally promote the same beliefs, and the redundancy would get rather boring. Needless to say, Osteen, like all Word of Faith teachers clearly promotes the heresies of *name it and claim it*, as well as a health and wealth gospel devoid of sin and repentance, which is really no gospel at all...

There are many other popular figures preaching Word of Faith doctrines today, so we'll just highlight some of the most popular ones, with the understanding that they all teach the same heresies we've already discussed; the next ones we will discuss have an emphasis on prosperity.

CHAPTER 3 The Prosperity Preachers

Creflo Dollar - A Word of Faith teacher with a special emphasis on prosperity. The following quote says it all...

"Jesus bled and died for us so that we can lay claim to the promise of financial prosperity." - Creflo Dollar on social media.

No, He didn't Creflo. Nothing in scripture remotely implies that Jesus was tortured to death so that you could get rich by lying about Him.

Dollar is also infamous for his shaky *proof* that Jesus was not God and was just a man. He refers to the scripture that says, *God never sleeps*, and then turns to the account of Jesus sleeping in the boat, before calming the storm. If Jesus was sleeping, that proves He wasn't God. This is nothing but theological ignorance and a dismissal of what the rest of scripture teaches on the nature of Jesus. He may have been asleep in His physical body, but in His spirit, He knew everything that was going on around Him!

John Avanzini - Here's a man who really knows how to twist scripture! Refuting the idea that Jesus was poor, he asserts that Jesus must have been rich, lived in a large house, and wore designer robes! This notion hangs on a very fanciful reading of scripture. In the first chapter of John, we see two disciples ask Jesus where he was staying. Jesus invited them to come and see. Avanzini twists this passage to imply that a huge multitude was asking this question, so if there was room for them to visit, it must have been a very large house! But when you look at the passage, it was merely *two* disciples asking the question! Judging by what we know of Jesus from the rest of scripture, He was probably staying with relatives, and surely there was ample room for that massive crowd of.... *two people!* As for Avanzini's claim that Jesus was rich, he refers us to scriptures that describe Judas as handling the money box. If Jesus needed a treasurer, He must have been handling big money! Designer robes? Sure, he finds that in scripture, too. Or at least he thinks he does...

"Jesus was handling big money because that treasurer He had was a thief. Now you can't tell me that a ministry with a treasurer that's a thief can operate on a few pennies. It took big money to operate that ministry because Judas was stealing out of that bag." – John Avanzini, Praise the Lord, TBN, 09/15/1988

"Jesus had a nice house, a big house–big enough to have company stay the night with Him at the house. Let me show you His house. Go over to John the first chapter and I'll show you His house. . . Now, child of God,

that's a house big enough to have company stay the night in. There's His house..."

"John 19 tells us that Jesus wore designer clothes. Well, what else you gonna call it? Designer clothes–that's blasphemy. No, that's what we call them today. I mean, you didn't get the stuff He wore off the rack. It wasn't a one-size-fits-all deal. No, this was custom stuff. It was the kind of a garment that kings and rich merchants wore. Kings and rich merchants wore that garment...

You don't think these Apostles didn't walk around with money? I mean, they had money. I just thank God that I saw this and gave up the denominational line and got on God's line before I starved me and all my family to death. Go to Acts 24. I mean. You don't think there wasn't money in this Paul's life! ... Paul had the kind of money that people, that government officials, would, would block up justice to try to get a bribe out of old Paul." – John Avanzini, Believer's Voice of Victory, TBN, 01/2010

John Hagee - Hagee usually comes across as an old-fashioned, biblical, fundamentalist preacher, yet he is one of the most egregious scripture twisters regarding money, tithing, and prosperity I've ever seen. Here's a passage of scripture he frequently twists and abuses regarding the subject from Malachi:

Malachi 3:8-12 Updated American Standard Version (UASV)

[8] Will a human dare to rob God? Yet you are robbing me! And you say, 'How have we robbed you?' In the tenth parts[30] and the offerings [9] You are cursed with a curse, for you are robbing me, the whole nation of you. [10] Bring all the tenth parts[31] into the storehouse, that there may be food in my house. And thereby put me to the test, says Jehovah of armies,[32] if I will not open the windows of heaven for you and pour down for you a blessing until there is nothing lacking. [11] I will rebuke the devourer for you,

---

[30] I.e. *tithes*

[31] I.e. *the full tithe*. The Mosaic Law was eliminated by Jesus' death, so monetary tithing is no longer a requirement. However, tithing has a figurative meaning. (Eph. 2:15) It does not symbolize the giving of our all. While the tenth part was brought every year, Christians now bring their all to the Father only once, when they dedicate themselves to him and symbolize their dedication by being water in water. It is whatever our situations allow, and our heart motivates us to use. The offerings we bring to the Father can be time, energy, and resources used in our carrying out the will of the Father, which would include attending Christian meetings, visiting sick ones and the elderly believers, and offering whatever financial support our heart moves us to give to God.

[32] **Jehovah of armies**: (Heb. *jhvh tsaba*) literally means an army of soldiers, or military forces (Gen. 21:22; Deut. 20:9). It can also be used figuratively, "the sun and the moon and the stars, all the armies of heaven." (Deut. 4:19) In the plural form, it is also used of the Israelites forces as well. (Ex. 6:26; 7:4; Num. 33:1; Psa. 44:9) However, the "armies" in the expression "Jehovah of armies" is a reference to the angelic forces primarily, if not exclusively.

so that it will not destroy the fruits of your soil, and your vine in the field will not fail to bear, says Jehovah of armies. ¹² Then all nations will call you blessed, for you will be a land of delight, says Jehovah of armies.

> **3:8.** In verses 8–12 we have Malachi's treatise on tithing, probably the most familiar passage in the book. Malachi's opening question is shocking—**Will a man rob God?** Even most unbelievers would be too frightened (if merely out of superstition) to steal from God. Yet, in addition to all their other offenses, the people were now charged with this heinous crime. Understandably, they wanted God to explain, **How do we rob you?** God replied, **In tithes and offerings.** The word tithe (also v. 10) is a translation of the Hebrew word ma'aser, which literally means "tenth part," defining the tithe as 10 percent of one's material increase. Offering is a more general term, specifying contributions for a sacred purpose. Tithes were given to support the priests and Levites, since the tribe of Levi received no allotment in the land of Canaan like the other tribes (Num. 18:21,24–29).
>
> **3:9–12.** As a result of Judah's sin, **the whole nation was under the curse** outlined in Deuteronomy 28:15–42—drought, poor crops, and so forth. The remedy was to **bring the whole tithe into the storehouse.** The words "the whole tithe" may intimate that some people were giving a partial tithe. The phrase **food in my house** (the temple) refers to the provisions for the priests' sustenance and the offerings. Tithing can be a frightening commitment. "How will we ever survive financially if we give so much to God? Our children will starve!" To allay such fears, God challenged Judah (and us) to test him in this matter. In other words, God says, "Give tithing a try and see what happens."
>
> If the people would trust him in the matter of tithing, God promised to lift the curse and send **so much blessing that you will not have room enough for it.** Rain would fall (heaven's **floodgates** opened), and they would have bountiful crops (not **room enough** to store it all). God would **prevent pests** (literally, "will rebuke the devourer"; probably locusts, Deut. 28:38) from destroying the grain, and the **vines** would produce abundantly. Even pagan **nations** would observe God's blessing on Judah and label it a **delightful land** (cp. Isa. 62:4). No doubt God blesses people spiritually when they obey him, but here we see that God often blesses us economically as well.³³
>
> **CPH NOTE:** The historical setting was the importance of tithes to the nation of Israel. They were the evidence that showed their appreciation on the part of the one giving to God and the nation as a

---

³³ Miller, Stephen. Holman Old Testament Commentary - Nahum-Malachi: 20 (Holman Old Testament Commentary) (p. 357-358). B&H Publishing Group.

> whole. This was their way of supporting true worship in a material way. Ephesians 2:15 tells us that the Mosaic Law was abolished on the basis of Jesus' death, so from the moment that Jesus offered his life as a ransom sacrifice in 33 C.E., mandatory monetary tithing at ten percent was not a requirement. The material offering that we bring to God now is whatever our circumstances permit, and our heart impels us to make. We must not forget that we can also offer our time and energy as well.

Those are some pretty stern words from Malachi, which Hagee and others use to their full advantage, but let's look at the passage in context. The Levitical Priesthood was in operation at the time, which created a unique set of circumstances. The priests were totally dedicated to serving God; they were not allowed to own land or grow crops. Therefore, the people were commanded to bring in a tenth of their crops and meats, so that the priests could eat! The tithe was not even monetary, it was food! Today, the Levitical system has been done away with, and likewise the command to tithe. It is truly disheartening to see how men like Hagee even use these verses to threaten people that *God will curse them if they don't tithe.* It's spiritual abuse. People feel obligated to give their ten percent and then some, and pastors like Hagee are reaping the rewards - not their congregants! This is standard practice for Word of Faith teachers, and some - like Kenneth Copeland - are buying private planes and mansions as a result. Their congregations; not so much.

Certainly, we should give generously to our local churches; the utility bills and so forth need to be paid, but we should give as the New Testament teaches, gladly and not under compulsion.

2 Corinthians 9:7 Updated American Standard Version (UASV)

⁷ Each one must give as he has decided in his heart, not reluctantly or under compulsion, for God loves a cheerful giver.

Nothing in the New Testament commands believers to tithe in a legalistic fashion. Rather, we are told to give as we decide in our hearts, out of generosity rather than obligation.

> **9:7.** In light of this wise saying, Paul encouraged the Corinthians to give. As before, he did not want them to give beyond their means, and the exact amount was a matter of conscience. The reliance on inward conviction in this matter is particularly important because Paul had no directive from God. As in every ethical choice that believers must make, there comes a point when the inward conviction of the Spirit must guide specific actions. Decisions of the heart must not violate the revelation of

> God, but they are necessary for practical application of the principles derived from the Old and New Testaments.
>
> Acting according to conscience was very important in this situation. Paul wanted the Corinthians to receive God's blessings in response to their generosity, but this would not occur if they gave **reluctantly or under compulsion** because **God loves a cheerful giver**. Once again, Paul relied on proverbial wisdom. This proverb probably circulated widely among Jewish rabbis and early Christian teachers because Paul used it freely as justification for his view. Paul believed that God's love extends to all who are in Christ, but he had in mind here a special affection or approval that leads to significant blessings in the life of the believer.[34]

There is no requirement to give any specific amount. False teachings on tithing are standard fare for all the Word of Faith teachers we've looked and have yet to meet.

Hagee's sermons generally sound solid to the point that it can be hard to spot his heresies. Aside from manipulative tithe-twisting, and the usual Word of Faith nonsense, (which he buries is a sea of *orthodox sounding* verbiage) his most damnable heresy is his teaching that Jesus never claimed to be the Messiah to the Jews. Yes, he actually says that the Jews will be saved by keeping the Old Testament Law, *(something scripture says no one can do!)* and that they should not be considered guilty of rejecting Jesus as Messiah, since He never claimed that He was! Let's just consider that in the light of this passage from Luke 4...

Luke 4:16-21 Updated American Standard Version (UASV)

¹⁶ And he came to Nazareth, where he had been brought up; and as was his custom, he went to the synagogue on the Sabbath day, and he stood up to read. ¹⁷ And the scroll[35] of the prophet Isaiah was given to him. And he unrolled the scroll[36] and found the place where it was written,

¹⁸ "The Spirit of the Lord is upon me,
 because he has anointed me
 to proclaim good news[37] to the poor.
He has sent me to proclaim release to the captives
 and recovering of sight to the blind,

---

[34] Richard L. Pratt Jr, *I & II Corinthians*, vol. 7, Holman New Testament Commentary (Nashville, TN: Broadman & Holman Publishers, 2000), 405.

[35] Or a *roll*
[36] Or *roll*
[37] Or *the gospel*

to set free those who are oppressed,
¹⁹ to proclaim the favorable year of the Lord."

²⁰ And he rolled up the scroll[38] and gave it back to the attendant and sat down; and the eyes of all in the synagogue were fixed on him. ²¹ And he began to say to them, "Today this Scripture has been fulfilled in your hearing."

Jesus here is reading a key messianic prophecy from the Book of Isaiah and affirming that He is the fulfillment of it.

And from John 4…

John 4:25-26 Updated American Standard Version (UASV)

²⁵ The woman said to him, "I know that Messiah is coming," (the one who is called Christ). When he comes, he will declare to us all things." ²⁶ Jesus said to her, "I who speak to you am he."

In this passage, which recounts Jesus' encounter with the woman at the well, she refers to prophecies regarding the coming of the Messiah. Jesus unequivocally responds that He is the promised Messiah.

And from Matthew…

Matthew 15:24 Updated American Standard Version (UASV)

²⁴ But he answered and said, "I was sent only to the lost sheep of the house of Israel."

Jesus here definitely states that He was sent to be the Messiah to the Jews. Later in Scripture, Paul will affirm that the gospel was proclaimed first to the Jews and then to the gentiles.

And the clincher, from Mark 14…

Mark 14:60-62 Updated American Standard Version (UASV)

⁶⁰ Then the high priest stood up in their midst and questioned Jesus, saying, "Do you say nothing in reply? What is it these men are testifying against you?" ⁶¹ But he kept silent and made no reply at all. Again the high priest began to question him and said to him, "Are you the Christ the Son of the Blessed One?" ⁶² Then Jesus said, "I am; and you will see the Son of Man sitting at the right hand of power and coming with the clouds of heaven."

---

[38] Or *roll*

These verses are taken from the account of Jesus' trial before the high priest, where he was directly asked if He was the Christ, the Messiah. Given Jesus' unmistakably affirmative answer, it is unfathomable how someone like Hagee could deny the fact that Jesus was indeed the Messiah to the Jews.

And from John Hagee...

"Jesus did not come to Earth to be the Messiah, . . . since Jesus refused by word and deed to claim to be the Messiah how can the Jews be blamed for rejecting what was never offered?" - John Hagee

I would love to hear Hagee explain his position in light of Mark 14:62. Is there still any doubt that he is a false teacher?

Oral Roberts - Refocusing on money, we need to pause and look at the deceptive doctrine of *seed faith*, popularized by Oral Roberts (1918-2009). Once again, we

must separate truth from error. Scripture does support the idea that God rewards generous giving. However, Word of Faith teachers have contorted this idea into a formula for self-enrichment. Let's look at a passage from Luke 6, which they twist to that end...

Luke 6:37-38 Updated American Standard Version (UASV)

[37] "Do not judge, and you will not be judged; and do not condemn, and you will not be condemned; pardon,[39] and you will be pardoned. [38] give, and it will be given to you. Good measure, pressed down, shaken together, running over, will be put into your lap. For with the measure that you are measuring out, they will measure out to you in return."

Jesus here is speaking of mercy and forgiveness. Give those things to others and they will be given to you.

6:37–38. Perhaps you had a different job description in mind when you decided to follow Jesus. You would join him in judging the world. You would point out all the evil people to God so he could give them what they deserve. God's ways are different. You experienced them from him. No judgment. No condemnation. No heaping punishment on others. Forgive! Give! Use fair, generous measuring cups to sell something to someone else.

---

[39] Lit *release*

> Yes, be generous in what you give to others. God will give you the same kind of measure you give others.[40]

Mark 10:28-31 Updated American Standard Version (UASV)

[28] Peter began to say to him, "Behold, we have left everything and followed you." [29] Jesus said, "Truly, I say to you, there is no one who has left house or brothers or sisters or mother or father or children or fields, for my sake and for the gospel's sake, [30] who will not receive a hundredfold now in this time, houses and brothers and sisters and mothers and children and fields, with persecutions, and in the age to come eternal life. [31] But many who are first will be last, and the last first."

> **10:28.** It is natural for us to wonder if our sacrifices have been noticed. Peter, the spokesman of the group and most likely the narrative voice behind this Gospel, reminded Jesus of just how much he and the others had given up to follow him.
>
> **10:29–30.** If Peter wanted affirmation that the disciples' sacrifices had been noticed, Jesus gave him that reassurance in this verse. There is no material possession that has been left behind that will not be repaid in this life or in the life to come. Many followers of Christ have lost families, but they have found new family members within the body of Christ.
>
> The addition of the word **persecutions** "remove the whole matter from the world of *quid pro quo*. They take away the idea of a material reward for a material sacrifice. They tell us of two things. They speak of the utter honesty of Jesus. He never offered an easy way. He told men straight that to be a Christian is a costly thing. Second, they tell us that Jesus never used a *bribe* to make men follow him. He used a *challenge*" (Barclay, *Mark*, p. 250).
>
> **10:31.** While many interpreters see this as a warning to Peter against pride in his own sacrifices, it seems to be more than that. Jesus had talked much during his journey to Jerusalem about the reversals in the kingdom. The outcasts are to be sought after and not hindered; the greatest must serve. This verse caps Jesus' teaching on wealth and reiterates his teaching not to judge by externals and surface appearances.[41]

---

[40] Trent C. Butler, *Luke*, vol. 3, Holman New Testament Commentary (Nashville, TN: Broadman & Holman Publishers, 2000), 93.

[41] Rodney L. Cooper, *Mark*, vol. 2, Holman New Testament Commentary (Nashville, TN: Broadman & Holman Publishers, 2000), 169.

Most biblical scholars whom I've researched say that in this passage, Jesus is promising those who follow Him that their needs will be met, and that they will be rewarded if not in this life, in the next. (The prosperity preachers also like to omit the part about receiving persecutions, since it poses an inconvenience to their narrative.)

Gloria Copeland claims that the meaning is as follows: If you give one dollar, God will give you one hundred dollars back, give ten dollars and get one thousand back, and so on according to the math. She goes on to enthuse that Mark 10:30 is a, *"very good deal!"* Such Scripture twisting could almost be laughable if it wasn't having such a devastating impact on those who believe it. Faithful followers of the Copelands and others of their ilk are habitually sending their tithes and offerings, sometimes even using their credit cards, and can't understand why God hasn't delivered on His end of the bargain yet. Meanwhile, the Copelands build on to their mansion and buy another jet. It is simply evil.

Mike Murdock- One of the most disturbing characters I've ever seen lie in the name of God, Murdock could be the subject of a book all by himself. As I've said before, some false teachers may sincerely believe what they teach, while others are deliberate cons. I'm pretty sure Mike Murdock is one of the latter. This man's entire *ministry* - and I use the term loosely - revolves around money. His broadcasts are nothing but appeals for money - with the promise of riches and miracles in return - so that he can stay on the air and spread the gospel. The ironic thing is that you will never hear him preach the gospel. If you watch him one hundred times, you will be encouraged to give money - and lots of it - well over one hundred times, and you will never once hear the gospel. His favorite trick is relating how he's *heard from the Lord* that if you give *an uncommon seed gift* of - say - one thousand dollars in the next thirty minutes, God will reward you with miracles of money, health, and restored relationships. It baffles me that more people can't see through this. He is also kind enough to assure his viewers that if they don't have one thousand dollars handy, the Holy Spirit told him it's OK to put it on a credit card! I can't fathom how the man sleeps at night.

"...the most beautiful thing on earth, is a hundred-dollar bill. I ain't seen a woman on earth as good looking as a hundred-dollar bill. There's something about that hundred-dollar bill that excites ya." - Mike Murdock

Rod Parsley - Like Murdock, Parsley is all about the money. He has a habit of taking a verse like this one...

2 Corinthians 8:9 Updated American Standard Version (UASV)

9 For you know the grace of our Lord Jesus Christ, that though he was rich, yet for your sake he became poor, so that you by his poverty might become rich.

...and manipulating it to tell viewers how blessed they'll be if they send in a "seed gift" of, say - $2,890.00 or $289.00 or.... you get the gist.

> "Though he was rich" means that Christ did not exploit his status for his own advantage. Instead, he relinquished that status to serve others (Phil 2:6). His riches "describe that estate of the pre-existent Christ which elsewhere in the New Testament is presented as 'the glory which I had with thee before the world was made'" (John 17:5), or as "being in the form of God" and having "equality with God" (Phil 2:6). ...
>
> It is far more likely that "he became poor" is an ingressive aorist that refers to the incarnation, the state Christ assumed in taking on this mortal life. Becoming poor refers to his "emptying himself" (Phil 2:6; see also Rom 15:3; Heb 12:2) and suggests that this is something he did voluntarily. Schelkle comments: "Christ renounced the divine fullness of power in which he dwelt with the Father, abandoned the heavenly glory which was his as the Son of God. He chose the poverty of human existence so that through his poverty he could impart the eternal riches of redemption to the poverty of all for whose sake he became poor." But how does this make us rich? Paul must also be thinking of Christ's death on the cross: "Christ became 'poor' by accepting the radical impoverishment of a degrading and humiliating death in which everything was taken from him."[49] Christ's incarnation climaxed in his death, and the principle of interchange—he became poor; we became rich—is the same as in 5:21: "Jesus gave up his righteousness (becoming 'sin') in order that believers might become the 'righteousness of God.'"[42]

Paula White - Word of Faith, and very little difference between her tactics and those of Murdock and Parsley. She's another one who likes to twist biblical chapter and verse divisions into how much one should send to her so-called ministry. Want a John 3:16 blessing? Send $3,160.00...or if you're poor send $316.00, etc. She's also well known for saying that *anyone who tells you to deny yourself is from Satan.* Maybe she forgot about this verse - from the mouth of Jesus...

Luke 9:23 Updated American Standard Version (UASV)

23 And he was saying to them all, "If anyone wants to come after me, let him disown himself, and take up his cross day after day and keep following me.

---

[42] David E. Garland, *2 Corinthians*, vol. 29, The New American Commentary (Nashville: Broadman & Holman Publishers, 1999), 376–378.

Jesus here clearly contradicts Paula White, so her blatant disregard for scripture is rather obvious.

> **9:23.** Many of you have followed me from place to place waiting for healing and miracles, Jesus continued. You are seeking the wrong thing. Yes, I provide healing and miracles to those in need. Those are signs of God's power as he brings his kingdom to earth through me. But that is not where this earthly ministry leads. The final road you travel as you follow me leads to a criminal's cross. Not a gold cross on a chain that enhances the beauty of the wearer. Not a piece of art in a museum that enhances the reputation of the artist or brings awe to a young art student. Not a massive cross atop a cathedral that marks off a holy place. No! This cross is among the world's cruelest instruments of torture. You cannot wear this cross. You must bear it. You bear it to the government's place of capital punishment. It becomes for you the gas chamber, the electric chair, the lethal injection all rolled into one.
>
> What does all this mean for us today? Self-denial. Quit looking for miracles and healing. Quit centering your attention on things that enhance and please you. Focus on Christ. Let him create a daily relationship with you. Find out what he wants you to do every day. Do it! Do not expect to win popularity contests, fame, fortune, or success. Be ready to suffer the rejection, pain, and death he suffered. His lifestyle leads to that. Only as you lead this lifestyle can you learn who the Messiah really is. Only this lifestyle leads to eternal life in heaven. Take up your cross and follow him to the death. Then you will find he is the life.[43]

Benny Hinn - Here is possibly the most well-known Word of Faith celebrity with an emphasis on faith-healing, along with prosperity; it's also worth mentioning his notoriety for teaching that there are nine persons in the Trinity - which he got from the Dake Bible as well as the usual WOF heresies. *(Not to mention oddities like Adam could fly to the moon, and that women were originally created to give birth out of their sides)* Actually, it might be appropriate to discuss him later when we look at faith healers, but he is full on prosperity, with lavish mansions, jet planes, and a lifestyle to match. Not one to be outdone by his peers, Hinn is responsible for all sorts of grandiose claims, such as that Jesus was going to appear bodily at his meetings in Nigeria, and that if people would keep their dead loved ones at home, (as opposed to delivering them to the funeral home) and touch the corpse's hand to the television during one of his broadcasts, they

---

[43] Trent C. Butler, *Luke*, vol. 3, Holman New Testament Commentary (Nashville, TN: Broadman & Holman Publishers, 2000), 146.

would come back to life! To date, there have been no reports of success with this, although he has made claims of resurrections in third world countries - and of course, the video camera wasn't working at the time.

CHAPTER 4 Personal Experience with the Word of

Before we proceed further, I would like to share some personal back story on my own experience and introduction into Word of Faith, and how that experience caused me to have an extremely heavy and urgent burden to share with others just how false and misleading this movement is and the folly of getting sucked into it.

In the fall of 2015, I was going through a rather tough time with some chronic medical conditions. A good friend, with doubtless good intentions, invited me to a meeting being held by someone who billed himself as a *healing evangelist*. His name was Billy Burke, and to say that in the next eighteen months or so, that he caused my eyes to be opened to the deceptions of the Word of Faith movement would be an understatement.

(Though I had never heard of Burke at the time, I have since learned that he is a rapidly rising star within the charismatic / Word of Faith camps, with close connections to Kenneth Copeland, Jesse DuPlantis and others in that movement, frequently appearing with them at Eagle Mountain Church, an offshoot of Kenneth Copeland Ministries.)

But at the outset, I knew nothing, and so, on a chilly November night, I walked into a hotel conference room, and into my first encounter with the world of faith-healing, something nearly all charismatics, and virtually all Word of Faith teachers endorse. As we walked into the venue, I overheard people talking about their experiences and gushing about Burke, as well as other faith healers like Benny Hinn and the late Kathryn Kuhlman. I didn't know a fraction of what I know now, but I had read a lot of disturbing things about both of them, which we'll discuss in another section.

The service was conducted in a very particular manner, which I later found out was virtually standard procedure for healing services. There was a long period of worship music featuring songs that tended to focus on the Holy Spirit in a relaxing, repetitive, mantra-like fashion. It created an atmosphere that was nearly mesmerizing for expectation and belief, something I soon learned all faith healers bank on - literally.

After the singing, Burke took the stage and commenced pumping the crowd with

exhortations that they were about to witness all manner of miracles, signs, and wonders; "T*his is going to be a **miracle service!***" He then requested testimonies from people who claimed to have been healed in prior services. There were testimonies aplenty, yet none were very impressive. There were tales of deliverance from headaches, backaches, mood disorders and other unobservable conditions. This was the first red flag for me. Here was a man who claimed to operate in the same miraculous gifts as Jesus and the Apostles, exclaiming, "*Jesus is the same yesterday, today and forever,*" but was I the only one noticing a huge discrepancy between these healings, and those recorded is scripture? Where were the truly paralyzed, crippled, and visibly ill people being restored before our eyes? I wanted to keep an open mind but honestly smelled a rat. Also discomfiting to me was this phenomenon of being *slain in the spirit*. Why did almost everyone who went up front, fall back in a dead faint when he touched their foreheads? And why did it almost never happen to children, or to people who mentioned that they were not from charismatic traditions? Not to mention, why is the experience never, ever described in scripture?

After the testimonies, an offering was taken in which another oddity was noticed. After exhorting the crowd that they must tithe in order to be blessed, plus *sow seed* above and beyond the tithe to be really, really blessed, *the seed faith doctrine again*, he told the crowd to bring their offerings to the front and to wave their money high over their heads.(At one point he had the audience repeat after him, *"The tithe I owe, the seed I sow!"*) What happened to giving in secret like Jesus taught, so as not to be praised by men? I was starting to see a lot of psychological manipulation in this whole experience.

With the offering buckets stuffed full of checks and large bills, it was now time for those who so desired, to come forward for healing. Still trying to keep an open mind, I took my place in line. Once again, I noticed a lot of invisible ailments being addressed but the more serious cases were a bit troubling. One poor blind girl remained blind but was admonished to declare that she was healed in Jesus' name and to wait for her miracle to manifest. An elderly man with severe back pain remained in pain and was told he needed to go home and start acting like he felt better, so he could receive his healing. Many other cases where people remained unchanged, were told that they need to remember that *sometimes healing is gradual...* Where in scripture did Jesus ever say any such thing? Jesus and the Apostles healed observable diseases in a way that was instantaneous, verifiable, and left no room for doubt. Something seemed very amiss here. Nevertheless, I proceeded up to the front until it was my turn. When asked what my problem was, I described my issues. He firmly grabbed my forehead while shouting, *"Power!"* Unlike most of his prospects, I failed to be slain, but I did stagger back a bit; honestly, I could feel him pushing me - hard. I felt no different, but like so many others who experienced nothing, I was told that my healing would manifest if I just believed.

In the interest of full disclosure, I will note that there were a few cases where healings seemed to have occurred. There were testimonies of people who claimed freedom from cancer and other maladies. I certainly don't have all the answers for what takes place in these cases, but it was obvious that Word of Faith doctrines *(false teachings)* was being proclaimed, and we will see that the *appearance* of a miracle, real or not, does not validate the ministry of someone who contradicts scripture. Healings have been observed at the hands of Hindu holy men, witches, occultists, and pagans. Let's remember how we see in Exodus, that the royal magicians were able to mimic certain miracles of God. Scripture is clear that the enemy will deceive many people with signs and wonders, *(miraculous deeds)* all the while masquerading as an angel of light.

Billy Burke's story is that he, himself was healed of terminal brain cancer at the age of nine by celebrated faith healer Kathryn Kuhlman. I didn't know a lot about her, but I did recall hearing a lot of questions regarding her legitimacy from other Christians. So, in my efforts to learn more about what was going on, I felt compelled to do some research, and what I learned was not encouraging. Her ministry was rife with scandals, alleged healings that were disproven, and even instances where people died because they believed they were healed and stopped taking their medications. I have no idea if Burke's claim of being healed by her is true, but even if it is, it does not validate his unbiblical teachings and practices.

There was something about all this that just felt wrong to me. But at the same time, I didn't want to make a judgment without learning as much as I could. And so, I was compelled to search for the truth; I delved into the most intensive period of Bible study, prayer, and research of my life. Also, having noticed that the other preachers this man endorsed were all Word of Faith teachers, *(Kenneth Copeland, Benny Hinn, Joyce Meyer, Creflo Dollar, TD Jakes, etc.)* I felt compelled to study these people, and what they were teaching. And so, began my education into the deceptive world of Word of Faith, the modern charismatic movement, faith healing, revelations, signs, and wonders, etc.

There was a part of me that wanted to learn that Billy Burke was legit and that his teachings and practices were biblical. Sadly, none of my research was at all encouraging. Regarding faith healers, I investigated the people Burke spoke highly of, like Benny Hinn, and nothing I learned about him stood up to the light of scripture. His world - and that of every faith healer I researched - was one of mind control, hypnosis - and / or - possibly, demonic deception. I learned that people entering a Benny Hinn meeting were made to sit far in the back if they were wheelchair-bound, or visibly paralyzed, and then given no chance to go forward for healing. And this was someone Burke looked up to?

Burke absolutely gushed about Kenneth Copeland, calling him a "*great man of God, and a role model."* We have already looked at him, although at the time I had not yet done sufficient research to know what a blasphemous false teacher he was and is. Nothing I was discovering was making me any more comfortable with Mr. Burke.

As time went on, I was invited to several more Billy Burke services. His preaching was always the same message on having enough faith to get your miracle, and how God would prosper you if you sowed enough seed. I'll never forget one service where he said, "If you're right with God, you're gonna see it in your health and *in your pockets!* Who came here to get healed? *Who came to get rich?*" That last question disgusted me.

Looking back, although I didn't yet know that much about Word of Faith, it was clear that he was promoting it. I remember one message where he was talking about the power of spoken words, when he said something like, "*when you speak faith-filled words, you release faith molecules into the atmosphere, which activates the force of faith, which permits God to release His promises!*" Even prior to my research, that just sounded totally bizarre. He also made references to the coming *great supernatural wealth transfer*, a red flag for the teachings of The New Apostolic Reformation, a movement even more unbiblical than Word of Faith, which we will look at later. And it never ceased to bother me that he *never* preached the gospel! His meetings seemed more like entertainment events where people just flocked to see so-called miracles (most of which looked more like parlor tricks or mind control) happen. How could he call himself a *healing evangelist*, if he never evangelized? Of the several meetings I attended, I heard him make a passing reference to being born again *once*. And that included no mention of how one could become that.

One meeting, in particular, was one of the most bizarre services I had ever witnessed! The meeting was hosted by a local charismatic church and held in a high school auditorium. From the onset, the atmosphere was chaotic. During the initial worship songs, it appeared that more people were speaking in tongues than singing. Mingled with the music, was a cacophony of about one hundred people speaking unintelligible tongues, which I found very disturbing since scripture clearly states that no more than two or three people should be doing that at one time and that someone should be translating what was being said. Later, we will also address the fact that biblical tongues were actual foreign languages, not gibberish, or some alleged heavenly tongue. All the while this chaos ensued, I observed all sorts of strangeness. One elderly man in the front row was frantically jumping up and down like a human pogo stick, while others were running around waving banners or rolling on the floor, weeping and babbling. Others were parading around blowing shofars, which only added to the maddening din. Apparently, these people had little regard for Paul's instruction that everything should be done in an orderly manner.

What took place at the end was a perfect example of the fraud and deception that takes place in such meetings. An elderly woman in a wheelchair was pushed to the front, where Burke asked her what her problem was. *"I shake when I walk, I can't stand for long,"* she said softly, so softly that most of the audience probably couldn't hear her. You can assume that most of those present, seeing an elderly woman in a wheelchair, believed this was a person who was truly disabled. (Remember, she said that she *could* walk but with difficulty) Billy Burke threw his hands up in a typically dramatic pose and instructed her, "*Get up* and *walk to me!*" She slowly arose as Burke held his hands aloft shouting, *"How great!! How great thou art!!"* The crowd went wild, thinking they had just seen a miracle, and of course, Burke ate it all up. *"Ohhh!! Somebody better gimme praise!!"*

And there you have a perfect example of what goes on in so many faith healing services; fraud and deceit. People who are not actually disabled, but simply have difficulty with something, are persuaded to do that which they already can do, and it's passed off as miraculous. I saw cases where Burke would tell the crowd, *"Oh my! This man here can't see,"* when in reality the man had just told him he had *blurry* vision. Burke would then hold up two fingers and ask the man how many he saw; of course, the response would be two - he wasn't actually *blind!* Again, the crowd reacted as if they had seen a miracle, when in fact *nothing happened!* I saw this type of deception over and over and over again!

There are discernment ministries and respected scholars like John MacArthur who believe that these so-called faith healers are operating in the demonic and have the ability to impart demonic possession or oppression by the laying on of hands. *(Remember that a true believer cannot be possessed but oppression is possible.)* Some claim that what takes place in these services is more likely along the lines of mind control or hypnosis, something I also hold as plausible. Personally, I tend to believe that what takes place is a combination of psychological manipulation *and* demonic deception *(I'll discuss my reasons shortly).* The more I saw, the more I felt compelled to research...

Some Thoughts on Faith Healing

Is there any such thing as a legitimate faith healer? While there's no doubt that Jesus and the Apostles healed the sick and raised the dead, one can reasonably ask if this sort of thing still happens today. While God certainly heals today *(as He sees fit)* in answer to prayer - does He ever do it through individuals gifted to do so? The biblical point of view is that if He does, it must be rather rare, and take place in relative obscurity. My research into modern faith healers has revealed absolutely nothing to support their so-called anointing. All the well-known faith healers, such as Kathryn Kuhlman, (*scandals, a secret divorce and remarriage that she was later was caught lying about, disproven healings, etc.*) Aimee Semple Mcpherson *(various scandals, affairs, and died of a drug overdose)*, Peter Popoff, (*received so-called words of knowledge through a radio earpiece*) Benny Hinn, (*scandals, alleged affairs, financial improprieties, faked healings*) Leroy Jenkins, etc. have left a legacy of dubious healings, either disproven or devoid of verification, scandals, and outright fraud. Many of them have a habit of selling such questionable items as miracle spring water, anointed prayer cloths, and other cons. And we must once again note the enormous difference between these modern healings, and the biblical miracles. Scripture wouldn't be all that impressive if the only healings recorded were of backaches, headaches, pigeon toe gait and vertigo.

Excursion Is Faith Healing Scriptural? By Edward D. Andrews

Really, there are two different thoughts when it comes to faith healing: (1) the scandalous evangelist standing on stage healing some cripple, and (2) some person living through or receiver from some tragic illness or accident. We picture the little girl in the wheelchair in an audience that can move nothing but her eyes, as the preacher is walking back and forth on the stage ranting to the point of spit flying everywhere. Soon some attendant wheels the little girl onto the stage, where the priest shakes her, screaming to God, speaking in some unknown language (gibberish), in the end, the girl starts to move, and in minutes, she is able to get up out of the chair and walk, to the joy and tears of thousands in the audience.

Then, thousands of miles away, there is another little girl critically ill at home under hospice care. She has an inoperable brain tumor. She is in the last days of her life. Her church prays one night through the entire night, only to find the next morning the girl is taken back to the hospital because she has appeared to of made a turnaround. When they do a brain scan, the doctors find no traces of a tumor; it is as though she never had one in the first place. We can hear this hypothetical little girl's words, as her lips tremble through the tears, "The doctors were so stunned and could not believe it," she said through the tears. "I was supposed to be dead within the 48-hours, I was literally on death's door. Then it happened, I started to feel myself literally come back to life as it were. I should not even be alive, but God has chosen to save me."

Imagine the joy of those church members, the families of both children. Both are being hailed as a miracle from God.

What is Faith Healing?

The faith healers in the West, i.e., countries of Europe and North and South America, take place by evangelists or ministers of different denominations, but more so with those of the charismatic movement (e.g., Pentecostals). The faith healers claim that they are carrying out a similar work of Jesus Christ and his apostles, having the power of God move through them.

Of course, there are the "healers" from religions outside of Christianity, which is more in line with voodoo priests, witch doctors, medicine men and the like. These believe that evil spirits cause sickness and they carry out ceremonies to drive the evil spirits away. There are what is known as "psychic surgeons" as well, who literally carry out psychic surgeries" in places such as the Philippines. Then, there are those that claim that miraculous healings are from the natural forces that surround us and have nothing to do with any religion. We only mention these in passing, because this book is dealing with Christians, and claims of what appears to be miraculous faith healing within Christianity.

Does Faith Healing Work?

Many times, we have seen or heard a doctor on the news saying that it is a miracle that so and so is alive, and they have no explanation as to why. If asked specifically about their use of the word "miracle," they usually are not attributing it to God, but rather as an event that appears to be contrary to the laws of nature, which the religious regarded as an act of God. The doctor generally uses the word as a figure of speech. One thing is for certain; the faith part of faith healing is really at play here and not in the way one might think. We cannot say for certain nor can we prove that any person's recovery is because God intervened because similar recoveries have taken place with atheists and even those of the darker side of things, like Wiccans.

What we know about the human mind is so minuscule that it cannot even be expressed accurately. What we do know or think we know is like a piece of sand out of all the beaches of sand in the world, and it amazing and astounding, which could fill thousands of books. Now, try to imagine what we do not know. The effect of the mind on the body's health is similarly unknown. How diseases react to the mind is not fully understood either. However, all medical professionals will tell you that if the patient has the attitude that they are going to die and that they could never beat their disease, it takes place far, far faster than those that see the victory over the disease and fight as if they are in an Olympic game. Now, couple that latter person with the mindset of one of great faith in God. The real miracle here is the brain and the mind, a gift from God.

Is There Any Harm In Believing in Faith Healing?

If a person is charismatic in their belief, believing that whatever happens is God's will, or worse still that God will help the faithful regardless. While this positive attitude may help the body to stay the course for a time, this person might not see the need for a doctor. Truly, that question lies before us as well. If God is going to heal the person regardless, why even see a doctor? What is the purpose? On the belief that the person living or dying is predestined, and nothing can change the outcome, why see a doctor? This author is personally aware of a person who did not see a doctor for her cancer, and she eventually dies a horrific death, which some confused Christian minds would say that was God's will. However, the cancer she had could have been easily beaten through medical technology. What many ultra-religious persons are not aware of; medical science is a gift from God as well. The knowledge and understanding that enables doctors to cure and save people come from the human mind, which God created, and even in imperfection, we have the capacity to accomplish much.

Some Similarities Cannot Be Ignored

During faith healing services or healing prayers by the church for the sick, it is noteworthy that some "speak in tongues," with some even falling into a trancelike state, where they cannot move, but say they were ware of everything happening. If we were to get the complete picture in many of these services, it would be very similar to the fits and trances, which include the other religious healers, i.e., the voodoo priests and witch doctors. While the psychic healers believe that their healings are not like that of religions, yet the procedures and experiences are very similar to the end. The procedures ad experiences are very similar to Spiritism, which come from many of the ancient oriental religions. Let us take a moment and consider what the procedure and experiences were like when Jesus and his apostles healed.

Jesus Heals

When Jesus healed, we find not charismatic jumping around, emotionalism, no speaking in tongues, no rants and ravings, no fits and trances, and no emotional sermons beforehand. In fact, when Jesus healed someone there was no big scene, it was quite informal. The one who was sick might touch Jesus, or Jesus might touch him, but there was no shaking him or smacking him in the forehead. At times, Jesus just lovingly spoke to the person, and they were healed. – Matthew 8:14-15; Luke 8:43-48; 17:12-19.

When Jesus healed physical illness, the cure was not by mental factors of mind and body. On one Sabbath, Jesus entered the synagogue and was teaching, and a man was there whose right hand was withered. Jesus said him, "Stretch out your hand." He did so, and his hand was restored. Psychosomatic healing cannot cure a withered hand. Certainly, there is no psychosomatic healing when raising the dead, which Jesus did with Lazarus, who had been dead for four days. (Matt. 4:23; Luke 6:6-11; 8:49-56) There was not one person who simply made small improvements in their healing; he never failed, but rather Jesus fully healed every disease and every affliction. We never hear of words like "disappointment" or "deception" in connection with Jesus' healings. Even Jesus' enemies, the Jewish religious leaders complained, "What are we to do? For this man performs many signs." (John 11:47-48) Do we notice the differences?

If faith healers heal any today, in their connection with spiritistic procedures and experiences, we must ask what the source of this power is. The Bible made the following warning, which I believe we need to take to heart.

Deuteronomy 18:10-11 Updated American Standard Version (UASV)

[10] There shall not be found among you anyone who makes his son or his daughter pass through the fire, one who uses divination, one who practices witchcraft, or one who interprets omens, or a sorcerer, [11] or one who casts a spell, or a medium, or a spiritist, or one who calls up the dead.

The purpose of this publication is to protect the modern-day Christian from being contaminated by demonic spirit forces, which are under the leadership of Satan himself, seeking to stumble any in their walk with God. When we think of the modern-day faith healers and their practices that very much resemble spiritistic practices, are in no way similar to those carried out by Jesus Christ. The common sense of seeing through these fraudulent ones is further appreciated when we realize the purpose of Jesus' healing was completed in the first century and will not be seen again until his second coming.

What Was the Purpose of Jesus' Healing?

1 Timothy 5:23 Updated American Standard Version (UASV)

[23] (Do not drink just water, but use a little wine for the sake of your stomach and your frequent ailments.)

Here we see the Paul's closest traveling companion and friend, Timothy was suffering from some frequent stomach ailment. Paul told Timothy, "Do not be hasty in the laying on of hands," but rather to use a common medical treatment. It should be noted that the early Christians who personally witnessed actual healings, even the raising of others from the dead by Jesus and the apostles, did not view the gift of healing as some form of therapy. Moreover, they were not given the commission to care for the physical well-being of humanity.

They had another commission, one that Jesus carried out and assigned to every Christian just before his ascension, to proclaim the gospel, to teach and to make disciples. Jesus told Pontius Pilate the purpose of his coming to earth. He said, "For this purpose I was born and for this purpose I have come into the world, to bear witness to the truth. Everyone who is of the truth listens to my voice."–John 18:37.

Why then did Jesus and the apostles heal people in the first-century? The healings and other miracles served as a sign. The Jewish people had been God's chosen people for 1,500-years, and now God was choosing another way for humankind to approach him, i.e., Christianity. Thus, the healings and other miracles were a sign that Christianity was now the Way and the Truth. The apostle Paul wrote,[44]

Hebrews 2:3-4 Updated American Standard Version (UASV)

³ how will we escape if we neglect so great a salvation? After it was at the first spoken through the Lord, it was confirmed to us by those who heard, ⁴ **God also testifying with them, both by signs and wonders and by various miracles** and by gifts of the Holy Spirit according to His own will.

The primary focus of first-century Christianity was not miracles but the bearing witness to Jesus Christ. This is why Christianity grew from five hundred disciples in 33 C.E. to over one million by 125 C.E., less that one hundred years later. The miracles simply were the evident demonstration to the Jews that God had chosen another course of drawing close to him. After the Christian congregation was well grounded in the first-century, the gifts of the spirit, which included healing were no longer needed. (1 Cor. 12:27–13:8) What about those claiming to perform miracles today in Jesus name?

Matthew 7:21-23 Updated American Standard Version (UASV)

²¹ "Not everyone who says to me, 'Lord, Lord,' will enter the kingdom of heaven, but **the one who does the will of my Father** who is in heaven. ²² On that day many will say to me, 'Lord, Lord, **did we not**

---

[44] http://www.christianpublishers.org/the-jews-chosen-people

prophesy in your name, and cast out demons in your name, and **do many mighty works** in your name?' ²³ And then I will declare to them, 'I never knew you; depart from me, you who practice lawlessness.'

Rather, here is where Jesus said the work of the Christian would lie,

Matthew 24:14 Updated American Standard Version (UASV)

¹⁴ And this gospel of the kingdom will be proclaimed in all the inhabited earth⁴⁵ as a testimony to all the nations, and then the end will come.

Matthew 28:19-20 Updated American Standard Version (UASV)

¹⁹ Go therefore and make disciples of all the nations, baptizing them in the name of the Father and the Son and the Holy Spirit, ²⁰ teaching them to observe all that I commanded you; and look, I am with you always, even to the end of the age."

When the Bible was completed, thirty-nine books of the Old Testament and twenty-seven books of the New Testament, the Christian had everything they needed to get them to Jesus second coming. When we think of the videos of the Pentecostal Church and other Charismatic groups, and the jumping around, body jerking, speaking in tongues, trances, and faith healing, we must realize that this showy display of oneself is not for God. In fact, the apostle Paul identified the speaking in tongues (not ecstatic speech, gibberish, but rather speaking a foreign language), with the babyhood of Christianity. After mentioning that speaking in tongues would cease, Paul wrote, "When I was a child, I spoke like a child, I thought like a child, I reasoned like a child. When I became a man, I gave up childish ways." According to Paul's own words, the historical evidence of the book of Acts and second-century writers, speaking in tongues passed away. (1 Cor. 13:8-11) Please see Does God Step in and Solve Our Every Problem Because We are Faithful?⁴⁶

Therefore, these showy displays of oneself must come from a different source than the "gifts of the spirit" in the first-century. The source is spiritistic, not the Spirit of God. Thus, we need to heed the warning of the apostle John, "Beloved, do not believe every spirit, but test the spirits to see whether they are from God, for many false prophets have gone out into the world."–1 John 4:1.

God's Word is Alive

Hebrews 4:12 Updated American Standard Version (UASV)

---

⁴⁵ Or *in the whole world*
⁴⁶ http://bit.ly/2qLdxgN

¹² For the word of God is living and active and sharper than any two-edged sword, and piercing as far as the division of soul and spirit, of both joints and marrow, and able to judge the thoughts and intentions of the heart.

Nowhere in Scripture will we find a promise that we will receive an instant relief from sickness. However, while the Bible is not a medical journal, it does offer extensive help on health matters. People who obeyed the Bible's guidance on physical and moral cleanness were able to avoid diseases long before science ever had knowledge of germs. Then, if we were to apply the counsel on envy, jealousy, and fits of anger, we would avoid many stress-related illnesses, including strokes and heart attacks. – Proverbs 14:29, 30; 2 Corinthians 7:1; Galatians 5:19-23.

If we are not anxious but rely fully on God's Word in the times of sickness; we can have,

Philippians 4:6-7 Updated American Standard Version (UASV)

⁶ In nothing be anxious; but in everything by prayer and supplication with thanksgiving let your requests be made known to God. ⁷ And the peace of God, which surpasses all understanding, will guard your hearts and your minds[47] in Christ Jesus.

⁶ do not be anxious about anything, but in everything by prayer and supplication with thanksgiving let your requests be made known to God. ⁷ And **the peace of God, which surpasses all understanding, will guard your hearts and your minds** in Christ Jesus.

One day soon, Jesus will remove the selfish, violent, wicked humankind and these oppressive human governments, to rule the earth for a thousand years. The apostle Peter said that Jesus' miracles were "mighty works and wonders and signs." (Acts 2:22) They were "signs" of the truths that Jesus gave us, and they were "wonders"[48] of what God will do for humanity when Jesus' kingdom carries out the will and purposes of the Father to be done in all the earth. Envision the healing and restoration work that will occur.

---

[47] Or "your mental powers; your thoughts."
[48] The Greek word rendered "wonders" is *teras*, has the sense of any amazing or wonderful occurrence; especially used of something seemingly preternatural, i.e., exceeding what is normal in nature. (Bible Sense Lexicon by Logos) *Teras* appeals to the imagination, manifested as divine operations. W. E. Vine, Merrill F. Unger, and William White Jr., Vine's *Complete Expository Dictionary of Old and New Testament Words* (Nashville, TN: T. Nelson, 1996), 682.

Moreover, while there is a heavenly hope, there is also another hope,

The New Earth: The Earthly Hope

In the O[ld] T[estament] the kingdom of God is usually described in terms of a redeemed earth; this is especially clear in the book of Isaiah, where the final state of the universe is already called new heavens and a new earth (65:17; 66:22) The nature of this renewal was perceived only very dimly by OT authors, but they did express the belief that a human's ultimate destiny is an earthly one.[49] This vision is clarified in the N[ew] T[estament]. Jesus speaks of the "renewal" of the world (Matt 19:28), Peter of the restoration of all things (Acts 3:21). Paul writes that the universe will be redeemed by God from its current state of bondage (Rom. 8:18-21). This is confirmed by Peter, who describes the new heavens and the new earth as the Christian's hope (2 Pet. 3:13). Finally, the book of Revelation includes a glorious vision of the end of the present universe and the creation of a new universe, full of righteousness and the presence of God. The vision is confirmed by God in the awesome declaration: "I am making everything new!" (Rev. 21:1-8).

The new heavens and the new earth will be the renewed creation that will fulfill the purpose for which God created the universe. It will be characterized by the complete rule of God and by the full realization of the final goal of redemption: "Now the dwelling of God is with men" (Rev. 21:3).

The fact that the universe will be created anew[50] shows that God's goals for humans is not an ethereal [heavenly] and disembodied existence, but a bodily existence on a perfected earth. The scene of the beatific vision is the new earth. The spiritual does not exclude the created order and will be fully realized only within a perfected creation. (Elwell 2001, 828-29)

---

[49] It is unwise to speak of the written Word of God as if it were of human origin, saying 'OT authors express the belief,' when what was written is the meaning and message of what God wanted to convey by means of the human author.

[50] Create anew does not mean a complete destruction followed by a re-creation, but instead a renewal of the present universe.

God created the earth to be inhabited, to be filled with perfect humans, who are over the animals, and under the sovereignty of God. (Gen. 1:28; 2:8, 15; Ps. 104:5; 115:16; Eccl. 1:4) Sin did not dissuade God from his plans (Isa. 45:18); on the contrary, he has saved redeemable humankind by Jesus' ransom sacrifice. It seems that the Bible offers two hopes to redeemed humans, **(1) a heavenly hope**, or **(2) an earthly hope**. It also seems that those with the heavenly hope are limited in number and are going to heaven to rule with Christ as kings, priests, and judges either **on** the earth or **over** the earth from heaven. In addition, it seems that those with the earthly hope are going to receive eternal life here on a renewed earth as originally intended. The book of Revelation describes this future healing,

Revelation 21:4-5 Updated American Standard Version (UASV)

⁴ and he will wipe away every tear from their eyes, and death shall be no more, neither shall there be mourning, nor crying, nor pain anymore, for the former things have passed away."

⁵ And the One seated on the throne said, "Look! I am making all things new." And he said, "Write, for these words are faithful and true."

What we have learned within this publication thus far is that God performed miracles in the past, but they were the exception to the rule. Even during the 4,000 years of biblical times, miracles were not the norm, and many times hundreds of years passed without any record of miracles taking place. When we see a cluster of miracles taking place within Scripture, it was a transitional period, such as,

- Abraham being called to a new land,
- Moses leading the Israelites out of Egypt and slavery,
- prophets warning of a coming punishment for northern Israel and southern Judah,
- and Jesus establishing a new way to God through the Christian congregation, no longer fleshly Israel.

We have also learned that God does involve himself miraculously into humankind, but not as often as we are crediting him. When someone claims that a tumor miraculously disappeared, and a child was saved from certain death, we have to recognize rationally that thousands of other children died that same year from brain tumors. In addition, we have to accept rationally that some of the other "miraculous" tumor cases took place with atheists. Moreover, we have to admit that we have only a very minuscule understanding of the mind-body relationship. Finally, we can thank God for the wonderful body and mind that he gave Adam and Eve, which still seems so miraculous in our imperfect condition.

Lastly, we admit that there are times when God does perform miracles on behalf of humankind, but these are exceptional and are for his will and purposes. Let us offer a probable example. William Tyndale published his translation of the English Bible from the original languages of Hebrew and Greek in 1526 (NT), 1530 (OT). The Catholic Church, who sought his death for daring to make a translation, treated him like an outlaw. He accomplished his translation while on the run from the Catholic Church. Like Jesus, a friend with a kiss, Philips, betrayed Tyndale. He finished his translation while being held in captivity. "Tyndale was arrested and imprisoned in the castle of Vilvoorden for over 500 days of horrible conditions. He was tried for heresy and treason in a ridiculously unfair trial and convicted. Tyndale was then strangled and burnt at the stake in the prison yard, Oct. 6, 1536. His last words were, 'Lord, open the king of England's eyes. This prayer was answered three years later, in the publication of King Henry VIII's 1539 English 'Great Bible.' Tyndale's place in history has not yet been sufficiently recognized as a translator of the Scriptures, as an apostle of liberty, and as a chief promoter of the Reformation in England."[51] Tyndale brought us the first printed English Bible, which was the foundation for the King James Version of 1611. If the reader of this book were to read in detail of the life of William Tyndale, he would see the likelihood of God coming to his aid, to countermove Satan, so that we got the translation that changed the English-speaking world.

If we are to remain rational in our thinking, we need to grasp the fact that God does not always perform miracles when we believe he should or did, nor is he obligated to do so. As was stated earlier, he has greater issues that need resolving, which have eternal effects for the whole of humankind. There are far more times when God does not perform miracles, meaning that our relief may come in the hope of the resurrection. However, for his servants that apply his Word in a balanced manner, fully, God is acting in their best interest by way of his inspired, inerrant Word.[52]

---

[51] Greatsite.com
http://www.greatsite.com/timeline-english-bible-history/william-tyndale.html

[52] Edward D. Andrews, *MIRACLES - DO THEY STILL HAPPEN TODAY? God Miraculously Saving People's Lives, Apparitions, Speaking In Tongues, Faith Healing* (Cambridge, OH: Christian Publishing House, 2015), 48-68.

Slain in the Spirit

BY WHAT SPIRIT ARE THEY SLAIN?

Later on, we're going to examine all sorts of manifestations being attributed to the Holy Spirit and discuss whether these phenomena could truly be of God or not. For now, let's start with the most commonly seen one, that of being *slain in the spirit*. This is when a faith healer or other minister touches someone on the forehead, *(or performs some similar action; Benny Hinn is known for making dozens of folks topple like dominos, all at once, by waving his suit coat at them)* and they fall backwards in a dead faint, sometimes for seconds, sometimes for much longer. This has become such a common sight in charismatic circles, it is often taken for granted. But is it Biblical? Does scripture support it? I once asked a charismatic friend if she could defend the practice. She told me it was like when the soldiers arresting Jesus in the Garden fell backward when He identified Himself. But is it? Let's look at the scripture...

John 18:3-6 Updated American Standard Version (UASV)

³ So Judas brought the detachment of soldiers and officers of the chief priests and of the Pharisees and came there with torches and lamps and weapons. ⁴ So Jesus, knowing all the things that were coming upon him, went forth and said to them, "Whom do you seek?" ⁵ They answered him, "Jesus of Nazareth." Jesus said to them, "I am he." And Judas also, who was betraying him, was standing with them.

⁶ So when he said to them, "I am he," they drew back and fell to the ground.

Bear in mind that what we see here is an account of the very Son of God revealing His identity to a group of mere mortals; a far cry from any so-called faith healer laying hands on someone.

One of the clearest expressions of humanistic pragmatism is found in the idea that truth and morals depend on one's personal experiences. Instead of studying Scripture to see what God has revealed, the Christian humanist will base his beliefs on human experience.

One example comes to mind which clearly illustrates this problem. The following is a dialogue between Sam and Bob over the issue of being "slain in the Spirit."

Sam: "Oh, what a wonderful time I had last night in church! I was 'slain in the Spirit,' and I must have lain there at least an hour. When Kathryn touched me, I felt the electricity of the Spirit and it knocked me down flat. Wasn't it wonderful?"

Bob: "I am glad that you had a wonderful time in church, but I am not altogether sure that this 'slain in the Spirit' stuff is Scriptural."

Sam: "Don't be silly! Of course, it is true because I experienced it, and a lot of other people have experienced it too. And, it felt so good to be slain. Kathryn came by me and I reached out and touched the hem of her garment and down I went. What could possibly be wrong with that?"

Bob: "But where in the Bible or church history do you find this stuff? Aren't you concerned in the least if 'being slain' is true according to God's Word? We must not interpret the Bible according to our experience. Instead, we must interpret our experience according to the Bible. Wouldn't you agree?"

Sam: "I don't see what you are getting all hyper about. I know it is true because I experienced it. I don't have to run around and prove it by the Bible or church history. But I'll ask my pastor for the proof tonight, and I'll tell you tomorrow."

The Next Day.

Bob: "Well, what did your pastor say?"

Sam: "He told me that I should not talk to you anymore. He said that you are guilty of something called 'bibliolatry' because you think that the Bible is God."

Bob: "But I don't think that the Bible is God and neither do I worship it as God. But the Bible does tell us that what we believe and how we live are to come from it and not from human experience. I guess that he could not come up with any proof and just told you to avoid me."

Sam: "No, he gave me all the proof I needed. Being 'slain in the Spirit' is clearly taught in John 18:6 and Rev. 1:17. There! Does that satisfy you?"

Bob: "I don't really think that you can legitimately use those passages. First, let me ask you something. Was being 'slain in the Spirit' a blessing or a judgment of God?"

Sam: "It's a wonderful blessing! I know because I experienced it."

Bob: "But if this is so, how can you use John 18:6, when in that passage Jesus judged his enemies who were coming to kill him by knocking them down? Furthermore, they did not become unconscious. It was also a very unpleasant experience for them. Remember, this was not a worship service! Jesus did not touch them. As a matter of fact, in

> the Gospels whenever Jesus touched people or they touched him, no one ever got knocked down."
>
> Sam: "Well, I must admit that John 18 doesn't exactly prove my case but Rev. 1:17 does."
>
> Bob: "Sam, did you bother to look at the text at all? It isn't enough to quote a verse. You have to examine it. Was there a worship service going on? Did an evangelist touch him? If you read the text you will find that John actually fainted in fright. He was so frightened by the appearance of Jesus that he fainted. Are you going to say that whenever someone faints in fright that this is what 'slain in the Spirit' is all about? I thought you told me it was a pleasant experience. Did you faint in fright the other night?"
>
> Sam: "You are doing exactly what my pastor said you would do. He warned me that you would rob me of those verses."
>
> Bob: "But, Sam, all I did was to look at the context and the wording of those passages. Isn't this what we are supposed to do as Christians?"
>
> Sam: "I'm not going to talk about it anymore with you. I know I am right because I experienced it, and you could show me all the verses in the Bible until you are blue in the face and I still will not believe you."
>
> This illustration is based on an actual conversation. Sam did not know it, but he was really a humanist and not a theist. His own experience was the measure of truth. He did not need the Bible to tell him right from wrong or truth from error. It did not matter what the issue was. It could be tongues, worship, healing, salvation, etc. In all these issues his experience was ultimate—not the Bible![53]

John 18:6 is a standard charismatic *proof text* for spirit-slaying. However, I, personally see an overwhelming discrepancy between the Garden scenario and what goes on in a healing service. First, this is but one example from Scripture of what happens to the *enemies of God* when they witness His glory. *(The righteous tend to voluntarily fall forward out of reverence and fear!)* Secondly, it's a huge jump to say that the touch of a Benny Hinn, or a Billy Burke, or *any* ordinary human is on a par with the *very incarnation of Almighty God* identifying Himself! So, what does cause people to fall back in these situations? Could it be the power of God? A better question might be, would God's power manifest through a false teacher? You will be hard pressed to find people being slain in the spirit at the hands of anyone other than extreme charismatics of the Word of Faith

---

[53] Robert A. Morey, *The Encyclopedia of Practical Christianity* (Las Vegas, NV: Christian Scholars Press, 2004), 225–226.

variety. I have never seen it occur in churches that affirm the supremacy of God's Word over and above *experiences.* I have never heard of this happening in churches that preach the biblical gospel. Also, I have a hard time being okay with something that is never described in scripture and was never known as commonplace until the early twentieth century. If this is a true experience of God and something to be desired, wouldn't scripture say *anything* about it? We will see going forward that much of what goes on in the modern charismatic movement can reasonably be questioned as to whether it's of God at all.

Which leads me briefly back to my personal story. Let's go back to what I experienced at -thankfully - my final Billy Burke service.

It was not a healing service per se, but a Sunday service with his regular home congregation. But a Billy Burke service would never be complete without some sensationalism, so at the end he started walking down the center aisle, smacking the foreheads of whomever he could reach, and they all fell like dominos. By this time, I was totally convinced that he was a false teacher, so I silently prayed that he wouldn't come near me. Alas, he came right at me, *"You too sir! The anointing is for everyone!"*

I really didn't expect anything to happen as I had zero faith in his powers, but much to my surprise, I did black out just long enough that I had to fall back to my seat. I can't say for certain what I experienced, but all I know is this; for those few seconds when everything went dark, what I saw and felt was simply the very darkest utter blackness - a total absence of light or any semblance of warmth - I have ever experienced in my life. It was chilling. Only God knows if I experienced something of my own imagination, or if I was truly touched by evil, but it was anything but holy! What I tend to believe is that God allowed me to just ever so briefly experience something demonic, *(and then mercifully pulled me out of it)* so that my eyes would be opened as to what was really happening with Mr. Burke. Ever since then, I've had a burden to share the truth about false teachers, by writing things such as you're reading now. People need to be warned that this is *not* of God!

Even those who agree that faith healers and manifestations like being slain in the spirit are not of God, may never agree as to what does go on there. Some - like me - are convinced it's demonic; others think it's just the simple power of suggestion - group hypnosis. For those who are convinced that it's *not* demonic, I would just ask you to consider the following: *At these events, false teachings are proclaimed. A false gospel is promoted.* They use a lot of legit-sounding Christian terminology, but the Jesus they speak of is *not* the Jesus of scripture; it's the genie in a bottle Jesus, waiting for your spoken words to command him. Scripture warns of false teachers, promoting a false gospel with signs and wonders. Personally, I believe that is exactly what is happening with the extreme charismatic / Word of Faith movement, and The New Apostolic Reformation, which we'll look at shortly.

Kundalini?

When discussing whether or not manifestations such as being slain in the spirit are demonic, we should discuss something known as *kundalini*. *Kundalini* is a phenomenon observed in various eastern religions, such as Hinduism. First, let's look at a basic dictionary definition if it:

Kundalini - noun, Hinduism.

the vital force lying dormant within one until activated by the practice of yoga, which leads one toward spiritual power and eventual salvation.

It is also referred to as the *serpent spirit*, that lays dormant at the base of the spine until released through yoga, meditation, or the touch of a *holy man*. When this *serpent spirit* is released, people display one or more of the following manifestations:

- *People fall backward and often report entering a trance.*
- *People report visions and revelations, sometimes claiming to travel in the spirit to other realms.*
- *People begin to shake, laugh or weep uncontrollably.*
- *People begin to speak in tongues other than known languages.*
- *These manifestations can be transferred to others by touch.*

Sound familiar? Many Christians believe that what goes on in the extreme charismatic Word of Faith movement is this demonic kundalini spirit, rather than anything to do with God. I can't be dogmatic about it, but it merits consideration. I'm talking about situations where a definite false gospel is proclaimed, along with questionable signs and wonders. Satan is a master of deception. Considering that self-control is a fruit of the Spirit, would self-control look like people falling to the floor twitching and jerking? Would self-control look like people barking, or making other animal sounds? Would self-control look like people screaming as if in pain, or babbling gibberish with no interpretation? I don't think so, and while I can't be dogmatic about it, it deserves serious thought. I have seen videos - which can easily be found online - of services conducted by Hindu holy men, that look disturbingly familiar. People line up to have the holy man touch them on the forehead, usually for healing or spiritual enlightenment; when he touches them, they tend to fall backward, shake, convulse, laugh or cry uncontrollably, speak in unknown tongues, etc. Sound familiar?

Again, without being dogmatic, I would just ask that you think about why these things were not commonly seen in the church until the early nineteen hundreds yet have been observed in eastern religions for thousands of years. Is Satan using the deceptive manifestations of kundalini to deceive people into thinking they're experiencing the Holy Spirit, and thus embrace a false gospel with no power to save them? I think it's quite likely. At any rate, the lack of control seen in such manifestations is surely not of God.

Some Thoughts on the Charismatic Movement

Faith healing is part and parcel of the modern charismatic movement, so we should spend some time discussing it. Few things in life are one hundred percent black or white and such is the case here. Yes, there are charismatic churches that operate biblically, but sadly, more and more of them are embracing Word of Faith and it's false man-made theology. If a congregation wants to worship with greater emotional expression than others, there is nothing wrong with that if solid biblical teaching is offered. But what we often see is scripture taking a back seat to experiences, feelings, alleged revelations, and an abhorrent abuse, or even disregarding of scripture. Keep in mind that experiences and feelings are subjective and possibly misleading, and that scripture is to be our final authority.

How can people who claim to revere the Word of God, promote so many doctrines void of biblical support? Part of the answer lies in an ideology known as *anti-intellectualism.* An alarming number of charismatics - especially in the Word of Faith camp, do not actually believe in serious Bible study! *(Of course, there are exceptions)* While many of them would deny that charge, the proof is in the pudding. Many of them that I've researched even say knowledge *(studying at the seminary level to learn what the Hebrew and Greek texts say)* is of the devil! Many charismatics are opposed to an in-depth education at the seminary level. They claim that if you have the Bible and the Holy Spirit, that's all you need. They'll claim that the apostles were uneducated men, a claim that holds no validity, as they learned from Jesus Himself, the very incarnation of God! And if they do go to school, they're likely to attend a school that simply indoctrinates its students into charismatic and Word of Faith beliefs, (like Hagin's Rhema) rather than digging into the Word to see what IT is saying!

Another source of such foolishness is the widespread belief that The King James version of scripture is the *only* authoritative and perfectly preserved Word of God. (Obviously, this belief is not held by *all* charismatics.) To summarize this mindset, King James Onlyists believe that no one had a trustworthy copy of God's Word until 1611 and that God must not care too much for non-English speakers. They offer a multitude of shaky "proofs" for their beliefs, and the subject could fill a book on its own. I would just encourage folks to consider how ludicrous it is to claim that even the oldest Greek and Hebrew manuscripts are less reliable than an English version that didn't come forth until thousands of years later. Did God not care enough for people who lived prior to 1611, and did not speak English to make sure that they had a reliable copy of His Word? KJV Onlyists claim that the King James translators were inspired by the Holy Spirit to produce the one and only accurate and perfectly preserved translation of God's Word, even claiming that all subsequent English versions are Satanic! I hope it is obvious how ludicrous that is!

Scholars who revere God's Word, take seriously the task of studying it. The original God-inspired texts were not written in English, and therefore simply taking the King James Version or any translation at face value can miss some nuances of what the original text is saying. Some Greek and Hebrew words do not have an exact English equivalent. Therefore, it is necessary to go back and examine the Greek and Hebrew texts. One key error resulting from not doing so is the belief that physical healing was purchased in the atonement. *By His stripes, we are healed!* As noted earlier, the Hebrew word translated as *healed* means *spiritual healing, not physical.* But for those who insist that a 1611 English translation is the infallible, authoritative and perfect Word of God, they are convinced that God wants everyone in perfect health all the time. Poor translations and misunderstandings of such words as those being translated as prosper, lead to another fallacy of the Health and Wealth Gospel, the notion that God wants us all rich.

The notion that God wants us all wealthy is one of the major reasons the Word of Faith movement is so popular. Who wouldn't want to hear that God wants to bless you financially and that there's a sure formula *(seed-faith)* to receive that gift? The sad truth is that what's being preached about prosperity is totally false and cannot stand up to the light of scripture. The Bible has far more warnings against desiring wealth than the Prosperity preachers like to acknowledge. Jesus said to his disciples,

Mark 10:25-26 Updated American Standard Version (UASV) Jesus tells us,

²⁵ It is easier for a camel to go through the eye of a needle than for a rich person to enter the kingdom of God." ²⁶ And they were more astonished, and said to him, "Then who can be saved?"

It is not difficult to understand here what Jesus is saying. Those who are consumed with the material things of this world will find it hard to give such things a backseat to the things of God.

Why then do prosperity preachers encourage their followers to seek earthly wealth? The answer is both simple and cynical; these false teachers are getting rich by lying to the poor. They tell people that they must tithe ten percent of their gross income no matter what and that they must give over and above the tithe to be abundantly blessed. I have read so many heartbreaking testimonies from people who gave these wolves their rent and grocery money, only to become poorer, while their favorite teachers bought mansions and private planes. The Prosperity Gospel prospers no one except the ones preaching it!

Have the Sign Gifts Ceased or Not?

This question has led to a great deal of debate, mostly between charismatics and non-charismatics. The issue can get complicated so let's try to strip it down...

First, let's look at the gifts of the Holy Spirit as described in 1st Corinthians...

1 Corinthians 12:4-11 Updated American Standard Version (UASV)

⁴ Now there are different gifts, but there is the same Spirit; ⁵ and there are different ministries, and yet there is the same Lord; ⁶ and there are varieties of effects, but the same God who works all things in all persons. ⁷ But the manifestation of the Spirit is given to each one for a beneficial purpose. ⁸ For to one is given speech of wisdom through the Spirit, to another speech of knowledge according to the same Spirit, ⁹ to another faith by the same Spirit, to another gifts of healing by that one Spirit, ¹⁰ to yet another operations of miraculous powers, to another prophesying, to another the distinguishing of spirits, to another different tongues, and to another interpretation of tongues. ¹¹ But all these operations are performed by the very same Spirit, distributing to each one respectively just as it wills.

The sign gifts are those gifts also known as apostolic gifts; healing, miracles, tongues, the interpretation of tongues and prophecy. Paul mentioned this in his second letter to the Corinthians...

2 Corinthians 12:12 Updated American Standard Version (USAV)

¹² The signs of a true apostle were performed among you with utmost patience, with signs and wonders and powerful works.

Note that the signs Paul is speaking of were the working of miracles, which were signs attesting to his apostleship.

It's worth discussing *why* Jesus imparted to the Apostles the ability to perform miraculous signs. Miracles were never an end unto themselves; they were performed to confirm that these men were speaking for God; to validate their message. It's important to note that the completed scriptures were not yet compiled in written form, so unless people saw confirming signs, why should they believe what the Apostles were proclaiming? This was the state of things as the Apostles were spreading the word and laying the foundations of the church.

Modern charismatics will say that Jesus is the same yesterday, today and forever, and therefore these gifts are still in operation. Cessationists say these gifts ceased with the passing of the Apostles, and the completion of scripture, thus the debate. In my opinion, neither side can *conclusively* prove their point by scripture, and so to gain some perspective we need to look at a combination of scripture, church history and real-life observations.

There will always be folks who point to tradition and anecdotal evidence, but just as the New Testament is chock full of miraculous deeds, after the Apostolic Age, reports of miracles became quite scarce. The cessationist view is that once God's complete and final revelation was available in written form, confirming signs were no longer required. Personally, I can't be dogmatic on this issue since God can do anything, anyway He sees fit. However, I lean towards cessationism with the disclaimer that if the sign gifts have not ceased, they have become extremely rare, and should not be expected as normative for today's church. As we explore this topic, we need to examine what's being labeled as *signs and wonders* today, and is there a point in history where the nature of the apostolic gifts changed?

It's worth noting again that the sign gifts were known as the *signs of an apostle.* Scripture relates the requirements for being an Apostle; they were to have been appointed by Christ and to have been eyewitnesses of the risen Christ. (Some people claim that Paul doesn't meet these requirements, but he does since Jesus appeared to him post-resurrection, and specifically commissioned him for his task.) With that in mind, no one today meets the *requirements* of biblical apostleship, therefore is anyone *qualified* to operate in the apostolic gifts today?

As noted earlier, reports of miracles all but vanished after the Apostolic age. The writings of those who succeeded the Apostles - the early church fathers - are mostly silent as to miraculous reports. Other accounts of church history have little to say about healings, tongues or prophecy over the last two thousand years. Suddenly, in the early nineteen hundreds, reports of tongues, miracles and new revelations began to abound. Were these the same Apostolic gifts as in scripture or was something else happening?

It is not my purpose to give a comprehensive history of the charismatic movement or to take an extremely scholarly look at the cessationism debate. Such books are out there if you want to learn more, so we're just going to skim over some significant points. A study of the charismatic movement in the early nineteen hundreds, reveals some movements with names like the Azusa Street Revival and Latter Rain. Within these movements, you will find reports of hitherto uncommon events, like being slain in the spirit or suddenly speaking in unknown tongues. There were breakouts of so-called *holy laughter.* There is an unfortunate story of some Americans who were suddenly convinced they were speaking Mandarin Chinese and believed they were equipped to go spread the gospel in China. They were quite dismayed when they got to China and found that no one understood a word they said. Therefore, proponents of this new charismatic movement moved the goalposts. Rather than admitting they'd been wrong about receiving the gift of tongues, they claimed it must be some heavenly, angelic language. Charismatics often say that a great revival and new move of God occurred with Azusa and similar events. Skeptics say it was more likely a counterfeit revival, a move of the enemy. As we proceed, I'll trust you to draw your own conclusions...

About tongues, we must note that the Greek word *glossolalia* - translated as *tongues* in the book of Acts means *languages*. The Apostles were not speaking something unknown; they were speaking the various foreign languages of their listeners...

Acts 2:4-8 Updated American Standard Version (UASV)

⁴ And they were all filled with the Holy Spirit and began to speak with other tongues,[54] as the Spirit was giving them utterance.[55]

⁵ Now there were dwelling in Jerusalem Jews, devout men from every nation under heaven. ⁶ And when this sound occurred, the crowd came together, and were bewildered because each one of them was hearing them speak in his own language. ⁷ And they were amazed and astonished, saying, "Behold, are not all these who are speaking Galileans? ⁸ How is it, then, that each one of us is hearing his own native language?[56]

This passage should make clear that the disciples were gifted with the ability to proclaim the gospel in the actual foreign languages of their listeners. This was not some mystical, unintelligible tongue.

It's worth repeating that when people claim to speak in tongues today, they are doing something very different than what took place in the book of Acts. Therefore, it's reasonable to ask if they are displaying the biblical gift of tongues or not. And again, those who defend the practice, say they are speaking in a private prayer language or some heavenly tongue. They

---

[54] *Or languages*
[55] *Or enable them to speak*
[56] *I.e. the language of his birth*

will point to passages like 1 Corinthians 13: 1, Updated American Standard Version (UASV) where Paul says,

13 If I speak in the tongues of men and of angels, but have not love, I am a noisy gong or a clanging cymbal.

Bear in mind that this is the opening to Paul's famous love chapter, where he uses several illustrations to point out the supremacy of love. Given the poetic language employed here, I find it reasonable to ask if Paul is talking about literal tongues of angels, or simply using a figure of speech to make his point about the supremacy of love.

There are also a lot of documented testimonies from ex-charismatics, who admit that they have faked speaking in tongues because there was so much pressure from their peers. It is also well known that many charismatics claim they can *teach* people how to speak in tongues; an odd claim if tongues are indeed a *gift* of the Holy Spirit. I saw a glaring example of this, courtesy of none other than Kenneth Copeland. On his program, Believer's Voice of Victory, he was telling his audience that all believers ought to pray in tongues for at least thirty minutes a day, and if they didn't it was their own fault. He then proceeded to tell them he was going to teach them how to speak in tongues so that they would no longer have an excuse. What followed was one of the most ridiculous things I've ever seen on so-called Christian TV. He said that the way to speak in tongues was to just start speaking anything other than English, and then the Holy Spirit would take over. He then said something along the lines of *babalaba babalabashabala babbaalaba and* declared that he had just spoken in tongues! All I'll say is, you'll have a tough time supporting his *tongues 101* lesson with scripture. And again, biblical tongues were real languages, not gibberish.

Related to the subject of tongues, is what charismatics call the Baptism of the Holy Spirit. They claim that being indwelt by the Holy Spirit is a separate and subsequent experience from being born again and is evidenced by speaking in tongues. This belief causes a lot of confusion since most non-charismatics have been taught that they are filled with the Holy Spirit at the time of regeneration.

According to scripture, the Holy Spirit most certainly indwells the believer at the time of belief:

1 John 4:15 Updated American Standard Version (UASV)

[15] Whoever confesses that Jesus is the Son of God, God remains in him, and he in God.

How else would God dwell inside the believer, except in the form of the Holy Spirit?

Titus 3:5 Updated American Standard Version (UASV)

⁵ he saved us, not by deeds of righteousness that we have done, but because of his mercy, through the washing of regeneration[13] and renewal by the Holy Spirit,

[13] **Regeneration (Rebirth), Born Again, Born of God, Born of the Spirit:** (Gr. palingenesiai; gennaō *anōthen*; *gennaō theos*; *gennaō pneuma*) This regeneration is the Holy Spirit working in his life, giving him a new nature, who repents and accepts Christ, placing him on the path to salvation. By taking in this knowledge of God's Word, we will be altering our way of thinking, which will affect our emotions and behavior, as well as our lives now and for eternity. This Word will influence our minds, making corrections in the way we think. If we are to have the Holy Spirit controlling our lives, we must 'renew our mind' (Rom. 12:2) "which is being renewed in knowledge" (Col. 3:10) of God and his will and purposes. (Matt 7:21-23; See Pro 2:1-6) All of this boils down to each individual Christian digging into the Scriptures in a meditative way, so he can 'discover the knowledge of God, receiving wisdom; from God's mouth, as well as knowledge and understanding.' (Pro. 2:5-6) As he acquires the mind that is inundated with the Word of God, he must also "be doers of the Word." – John 3:3; 6-7; 2 Corinthians 5:17; Titus 3:5; James 1:22-25.

The new birth comes from within. How else could the Holy Spirit renew us, except from within? Why then do charismatics insist that receiving the Holy Spirit is an experience separate from the new birth? It is because they are expecting something that happened one unique time in history to be repeated over and over; the day of Pentecost.

Acts 2: 2-4 Updated American Standard Version (UASV)

² And suddenly there came from heaven a sound like a mighty rushing wind, and it filled the entire house where they were sitting. ³ And divided tongues as of fire appeared to them and rested on each one of them. ⁴ And they were all filled with the Holy Spirit and began to speak with other tongues,[57] as the Spirit was giving them utterance.[58]

Prior to the day of Pentecost, God had not yet sent the Holy Spirit to indwell all believers. On that day, the Spirit was sent to indwell and empower them. Charismatics tend to point to other passages, where the Apostles asked certain believers if they had yet received the Holy Spirit, as evidence for their position. However, any scripture must be interpreted with the balance of scripture. When considered against the rest of scripture, it appears that those believers who were not present at Pentecost, received

---

[57] Or languages
[58] Or enable them to speak

the Spirit through the laying on of the Apostles hands. After this time period, scripture indicates that believers receive the Holy Spirit when they become born again.

It's worth noting here that, if speaking in tongues was indeed an evidence of receiving the Holy Spirit, then what about today? As a rule, we don't see new believers immediately speaking in tongues upon belief. At Pentecost, there was a valid reason why the Apostles were given the gift of tongues; to preach the gospel to those foreigners who were present. And again, the tongues spoken were real languages, not something unintelligible and unknown.

This leads to another question; when someone today claims to have received the Baptism of the Holy Spirit and begins speaking in unknown tongues, what is really happening? This is not something I can prove or be dogmatic on, but I personally believe that given the hyper-emotional nature of what goes on in charismatic circles, people possibly get so keyed up about receiving the Holy Spirit - even though they already have Him if truly saved - that they get swept up in the tides of emotion, and convince themselves that they are going to start speaking in tongues; as mentioned before, many have confessed to faking it. That is the most harmless scenario. The other possibility, where people have been led to embrace a totally false gospel, could be manifestations of demonic control. At any rate, what one believes about the Baptism of the Holy Spirit is not a matter essential for salvation. But given what we've discussed in the light of scripture and real-life observations, I would say that this belief in a post-salvation experience, evidenced by counterfeit tongues is a delusion. And given that people who experience this do not speak biblical tongues - foreign languages, I find that the whole discussion lends further credibility to cessationism.

It is not my intention to settle the debate regarding the continuation or cessation of the sign gifts, but in the spirit of discernment let's keep a few things in mind. God can certainly give any gift to anyone as He sees fit but do we see evidence of the *genuine* apostolic gifts operating today? Do we see spectacular miracles along the lines of paraplegics made to walk, or the instantaneous disappearance of disfiguring diseases like leprosy? Do we see any *verifiable* reports of the dead being raised? Do we see alleged faith healers going to hospitals, and curing actual sick people? Or, are we going to be content to label as *apostolic,* the remission of headaches and backaches, or believe that a faith healer can command a short leg to grow half an inch? (And isn't it interesting how every faith healer seems to find someone in their audience who needs a leg lengthened? Seriously folks - it's a parlor trick.) To conclude this section, I'll just say that I can't dogmatically say that the sign gifts have ceased, but I would say that the burden of proof is on the continuationists, to show us some evidence of *genuine* apostolic gifts operating today. And as a final note, I have yet to discover a faith healer who does not promote the heresies of Word of Faith theology.

> ### Is Speaking in Tongues Evidence of True Christianity?
>
> An extraordinary gift conveyed through the Holy Spirit to a number of disciples starting at Pentecost 33 C.E. that made it possible for them to speak or otherwise glorify God in a tongue in addition to their own.
>
> ### What Was the Reason for the Speaking in Tongues?
>
> Immediately before his ascension to heaven, Jesus told those who were looking on: "you will receive power when the Holy Spirit has come upon you, and you will be my witnesses in Jerusalem and in all Judea and Samaria, and to the end of the earth." (Acts 1:8, ESV) First, this witnessing campaign was to be of epic proportions; and second, it was to be brought about with the help of the Holy Spirit.
>
> Our modern-day world allows the spread of the gospel to the other side of the globe within a millisecond and in any language. In the first-century, the good news was spread either in written form, orally, or both. Therefore, the ability to be miraculously able to speak a foreign language in the melting pot of that Roman Empire would have been greatly appreciated. This miracle was first realized at the Pentecost 33 C.E. celebration, as the first-century Christians began to witness to the Jews and proselytes in Jerusalem.
>
> ### Acts 2:5-11, 41 Updated American Standard Version (UASV)
>
> ⁵ Now there were dwelling in Jerusalem Jews, devout men from every nation under heaven. ⁶ And when this sound occurred, the crowd came together, and were bewildered because each one of them was hearing them speak in his own language. ⁷ And they were amazed and astonished, saying, "Behold, are not all these who are speaking Galileans? ⁸ How is it, then, that each one of us is hearing his own native language?[59] ⁹ Parthians and Medes and Elamites and residents of Mesopotamia, Judea and Cappadocia, Pontus and Asia, ¹⁰ Phrygia and Pamphylia, Egypt and the parts of Libya belonging to Cyrene, and visitors from Rome, ¹¹ Cretans and Arabs, we hear them in our own tongues speaking of the mighty deeds of God." ⁴¹ So then, those who had received his

---

[59] I.e. the language of his birth

word were baptized; and that day there were added about three thousand souls.[60]

A major change was in the offing. The Jews had followed the lead of their religious leaders in the last act of rebellion, resulting in their rejection as his people. The Mosaic Law was being replaced with the law of Christ. This does not mean that no Jew could be received into the newly founded Christian congregation. To the contrary, the next three and half years would be only the Jewish people, who would make up this new way to God. As was the case with Moses, there was to be a sign, miraculous events, which included the speaking in tongues, this as evidence to those, whose heart was receptive to the truth that the Son of God had come, had given his life for them, and ascended back to heaven. Exodus 19:16-19

Speaking in tongues in Acts 2 is evidentiary. The unique speech is demonstrable proof that something supernatural has happened to the 120 disciples of Jesus. Tongues are the sign that these people have received the promise given by Jesus in Acts 1:5, "You will be baptized with the Holy Spirit not many days from now." This sign was clear enough so that all of those present for the Feast of Weeks was able to see that an impossible event was actually happening. The language speech in this chapter has a second, though subordinate, purpose—the communication of the gospel to people of a foreign tongue.[61]

However, there was much labor to be done. Beginning in 36 C.E., with the conversion of Cornelius, an uncircumcised Gentile, the gospel got underway in its spread to non-Jewish people of every nation. (Acts, chap. 10) In truth, so swiftly did it spread that by about 60 C.E., the apostle Paul could say that the gospel had been "proclaimed in all creation that is under heaven." (Col. 1:23) Consequently, by the time of the last apostle's death (John c. 100 C.E.), Jesus' faithful followers had made disciples all the way through the Roman Empire—in Asia, Europe, and Africa!

Spread of Christianity in the first century[62]

---

[60] I.e., persons

[61] Chad Brand, "Tongues, Gift Of", in Holman Illustrated Bible Dictionary, ed. Charles Draper, Archie England, Steve Bond et al., 1605 (Nashville, TN: Holman Bible Publishers, 2003).

[62] (Ac 1:8; 2:1-4, 11; 2:37-41; Ac 5:27, 28, 40-42; 6:7; 8:1, 4, 14-17; 10:1-48; 11:20, 21)

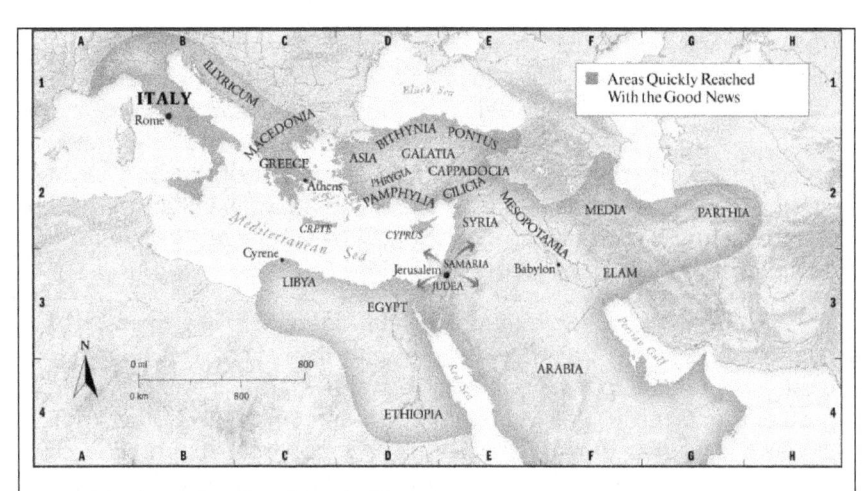

Modern-day Speaking in Tongues

Among those 'speaking in tongues' today are Pentecostals and Baptists, also Roman Catholics, Episcopalians, Methodists, Lutherans, and Presbyterians. Jesus said, "When the Spirit of truth comes, he will guide you into all the truth ..." Would the Pentecostals or the Baptists, who "speak in tongues" suggest that the Roman Catholics, who "speak in tongues" have been 'guided into all the truth,' by the Holy Spirit, as well as the other way around. If modern-day "speaking in tongues" is truly, the same as the first century, and it is evidence, proof that a person has Holy Spirit; then, all of the above groups would equally have to be the true path to God.

There is certainly mixed feeling over the revival of speaking in tongues at the beginning of the 20th century. Many see it as nothing more than excessiveness of unhinged persons, doing nothing more than drawing attention to themselves. On the other hand, many see it as the second Pentecost, identical to the occurrence of speaking with tongues in 33 C.E. There is a difference though for the modern-day counterpart where speaking in unknown tongues occurs. A rapturous explosion of jumbled sounds usually initiates it. Many who have been present at such occasions are unable to understand the chaotic speech, as is the case with all others who are present as well as the speaker himself.

Certainly, any reasonable person is moved to ask 'where the benefit in such unknown tongues is, and where the interpreters are?' It is true that there are some, who claim to interpret this incomprehensible speech, yet here again there exist credibility, because different explanations are offered for the same speech. In an attempt at removing this difficulty, they offer that God has simply given a different interpretation to these ones. However, they are unable to remove the stain that some of this speech has been base (that is, unseemly, unscrupulous, unprincipled, shameful, evil, sinful), degrading and depraved. Ronald E. Baxter, in his book *Charismatic Gift of Tongues*, mentions an example where a man refused to interpret the speech of a woman who spoke in the so-called 'gift of tongues,' saying, "The language was the vilest of the vile." This is hardly in harmony with the first-century Christian congregation, where tongues were used for "building up the church." 1 Corinthians 14:4-6, 12, 18.

Still, some have heard the interpretation of what they perceive to be a breathtaking message and believe with their whole heart that God is using this unintelligible speech to give messages to his people. The only problem with this is that Muhammad, Joseph Smith, and others make the same kind of argument. The book of Mormon is the supposed second testament of Christ for millions of Mormons. However, like the modern-day speaking in tongues, we are told very clearly not to go beyond what is written, do not add, nor take away, and that there would be no more miraculous messages until after Armageddon, where more books would be made available. Further still, what could be added to the unintelligible speech that is not available by means of Jesus Christ and the apostles through the Greek New Testament: "All Scripture is breathed out by God and profitable for teaching, for reproof, for correction, and for training in righteousness, that the man of God may be competent, equipped for every good work." 2 Timothy 3:16-17; Deut. 4:12; Gal 1:8; Rev 20:12; 21:18-19

As is quite clear from the New Testament itself, the gift of tongues was for a congregation that was in its infancy and was needed for the preaching of the gospel and the building up the church. However, this is no longer the case: "But even if we or an angel from heaven should preach to you a gospel contrary ["at variance with," *The New English Bible*] to the one we preached to you, let him be accursed."—Galatians 1:8.

Thus then, the gift of tongues is no longer needed, and there is no Biblical foundation for supposing that it is an element of modern-day Christianity. In fact, it is unlikely that it ever survived to the middle of the second-century C.E. At present, the Bible is whole and extensively obtainable, and the Word of God is all that we require. This book alone is a roadmap to an approved relationship with the Father and the Son, which leads to life eternal. John 17:3; Revelation 22:18, 19

The primary verse to consider reads, "For one who speaks in a tongue speaks not to men but to God; for no one understands him, but he utters mysteries in the Spirit." (1 Cor. 14:2) When considering this verse, he should keep verses 13-19 of the same chapter in mind.[63]

In other words, those who speak in a tongue speak to God as opposed to men if he does not have an interpreter for his speech that is to men who are listening. That is to say, the speaking in tongues is meaningless to the men listening, who do not know (understand) the foreign language as given miraculously through the Holy Spirit. It is for this very reason that Paul says, "no one understands." It could also have been that even the speaker himself of the foreign language did not understand what he was saying because he was not also given the power to interpret (translate). Therefore, without an interpreter, be it himself or another, his speech would only be understood by God, i.e., would be speech only to God, as opposed to men. This is why the apostle Paul would say that if there were no interpreters present, the one speaking in a foreign tongue, should also pray for the gift of interpretation as well. This is so he can also speak to men in a beneficial manner, as well as bring praise to God.

It is Paul, in the first-century, who through the Corinthian congregation sat straight those who had become spellbound and awestruck with the gift of tongues, behaving juvenile, young in the Spirit. While the gift of tongues had its purpose, these ones acted as though it was the most important aspect of the Christian church. (1 Corinthians 14:1-39) The apostle Paul made several things very clear: it was not even a gift that all possessed. Moreover, it did not contribute as an identifying mark of a true Christian or lead to salvation. Moreover, it was second to the gift of prophecy [proclaiming]. (Elwell, 2001, 1207) Therefore, this gift was not some marker that identified a person as a true Christian, nor was it required to receive the gift of life. 1 Corinthians 12:29, 30; 14:4, 5

What is the Real Force Behind Today's Speaking in Tongues?

There is no doubt that the charismatic church leaders of the 20th century are the impetus behind the resurgence of the speaking in tongues phenomena, pushing their flock members through emotionalism and coercion to achieve this alleged gift. This emotionalist duress is brought on by these church leaders, who exclude any who are unable to speak in tongues and treat the other members of the church as superior for their ability to speak in tongues. Therefore, the motivating factor is not the Spirit, not to build up the church, not the glorification of God, but to belong.

---

[63] http://biblia.com/books/esv/1Co14.13

Should Christians be identified by their ability to "speak in tongues"?

John 13:35 Updated American Standard Version (UASV)

[35] By this all men will know that you are my disciples, if you have love for one another."

1 Corinthians 13:1 Updated American Standard Version (UASV)

13 If I speak in the tongues of men and of angels, but have not love, I am a noisy gong or a clanging cymbal.

Jesus made the Great Commission all too clear when he said, you will receive power when the Holy Spirit has come upon you, and you will be my witnesses in Jerusalem and in all Judea and Samaria, and to the end of the earth." (Ac 1:8) He had instructed them and us to "Go therefore and make disciples of all nations, teaching them" (Matt 28:19-20). Moreover, he had earlier stressed that this was the last sign before the end of this age, by saying, "this gospel of the kingdom will be proclaimed throughout the whole world as a testimony to all nations, and then the end will come." (Matt 24:14) Do we see this being done by the charismatic groups, who advocate "speaking in tongues"? When was the last time you saw a Pentecostal come to your door, proclaiming the Good News? When was the last time you were out, and a Pentecostal witnessed to you? What Pentecostal church have you ever been to that has an evangelism program, to train its members to evangelize their community?

This gift of tongues is possible by mass hysteria. Worse still, the spirit directing this movement may very well not be the Holy Spirit. "She followed Paul and us, crying out, these men are servants of the Most High God, who proclaim to you the way of salvation.' And this she kept doing for many days. Paul, having become greatly annoyed, turned and said to the spirit, 'I command you in the name of Jesus Christ to come out of her.' And it came out that very hour." (Acts 16:17, 18) The apostle Paul cautioned, "Satan disguises himself as an angel of light." (2 Corinthians 11:14) By seeking a Biblical gift that is no more, these ones have made themselves possible victims of "the lawless one [who] is by the activity of Satan with all power and false signs and wonders, and with all wicked deception for those who are perishing, because they refused to love the truth and so be saved." (2 Thessalonians 2:9, 10) However, some might ask:

Does not Mark 16:17, 18 (NKJ) show that the gift of 'speaking with new tongues' would be a sign, so as to recognize believers?

Mark 16:17-18 New King James Version (NKJV)

[17] And these signs will follow those who believe: In My name they will cast out demons; **they will speak with new tongues**; [18] they will take up serpents; and if they drink anything deadly, it will by no means hurt them; they will lay hands on the sick, and they will recover."

First, there is the telling fact that two of the oldest and most highly respected Bible manuscripts, the Vaticanus 03 and the Sinaiticus 01, do not contain this section; they conclude Mark's Gospel with verse eight. This is true of the early versions as well: Syriac, Coptic, Armenian, and Georgian. The early church fathers, Clement, Origen, Cyprian, and Cyril of Jerusalem had no knowledge of anything beyond verse eight. There is little wonder that the noted manuscript authority Dr. Westcott states, "the verses which follow [9-20] are no part of the original narrative but an appendage." Among other noted scholars of the same opinion are Tregelles, Tischendorf, Griesbach, Metzger, and Comfort, to mention just a few.

Adding weight to this evidence of the Greek manuscripts, versions and church fathers are the church historian Eusebius and the Bible translator Jerome. Eusebius wrote that the longer ending was not in the "accurate copies," for "at this point [verse 8] the end of the Gospel according to Mark is determined in nearly all the copies of the Gospel according to Mark." In addition, Jerome, writing about 407 C.E. said, "nearly all Greek MSS have not got this passage."

The vocabulary and style of Mark 16:9-20 vary so drastically from the Gospel of Mark that it scarcely seems possible that Mark himself wrote those verses. Mark's style is plain, direct; his paragraphs are short, and the transitions are simple. However, in this ending, there is well-arranged succession of statements, each of them having proper introductory expressions.

Then there is the consideration of the vocabulary of Mark. Verses 9 through 20 contain words that do not appear elsewhere in Mark's Gospel, and some that do not appear in any of the Gospels, and some still that do not appear in the whole of the Greek New Testament. Verses 9 through 20 contain 163 Greek words, of which, 19 words, 2 phrases do not occur elsewhere in the Gospel of Mark. Looking at it another way, in these 12 verses there are 109 different words, and, of these, 11 words and 2 phrases are exclusive to these 12 verses. Moreover, the doctrinal thesis of Joseph Hug showed that when compared with the vocabulary of the other Gospels, the Apostolic Fathers, and the apocryphal literature, you have 12 verses in "an advanced state of tradition." The note at the end of Metzger's The Text of the New Testament, where I found a summary of Hug's thesis, states:

The vocabulary suggests that the composition of the ending is appropriately located at the end of the first century or in the middle of the second century. Those who were responsible for adding the verses were intent, not only to supply a suitable ending for the Second Gospel but also to provide missionary instruction to a Christian Hellenistic community that participated in charismatic activities... (Metzger 1964, 1968, 1992, 297)

The content of these verses also removes them from being considered as original. There is nothing within the whole of the New Testament, which would support the contention in verse 18 that the disciples of Christ were able to drink poison, having no harm come to them. In addition, within this spurious text, you have eleven apostles refusing to believe the testimony of two disciples whom Jesus had come across on the way and to whom he made himself known. However, when the two disciples found the eleven, their reaction was quite different, stating, "The Lord has risen indeed, and has appeared to Simon!" Luke 24:13-35

In summary, Mark 16:9-20 **(1)** is not found in two of the oldest and most highly regarded Greek manuscripts as well as others. **(2)** They are also not found in many of the oldest versions. **(3)** The early church fathers had no knowledge of anything beyond verse eight. **(4)** Such ancient scholars as Eusebius and Jerome marked them spurious. **(5)** The style of these verses is utterly different from that of Mark. **(6)** The vocabulary used in these verses is different from that of Mark. **(7)** Verse 8 does not transition well with verse 9, jumping from the women disciples to Jesus' resurrection appearance. Jesus does not need to appear because Mark ended with the announcement that he had. We only want that because the other Gospels give us an appearance. So we expect it. **(8)** The very content of these verses contradicts the facts and the rest of the Greek New Testament. With textual scholarship, being very well aware of Mark's abrupt style of writing, and abrupt ending to his Gospel does not seem out of place. Eusebius and Jerome, as well as this writer, agree.

Mark 16:17-18 New King James Version (NKJV)

[17] And these signs will follow those who believe: In My name **(1)** they will cast out demons; **(2)** they will speak with new tongues; **(3)** [18] they will take up serpents; and if they drink anything

deadly, it will by no means hurt them; **(4)** they will lay hands on the sick, and they will recover."

Is this really, what the Bible teaches?

While Paul was bitten by a poisonous snake and survived, we never find anyone in the New Testament going out to find poisonous snakes, for the purpose of handling them in a religious service. To the contrary, Paul quickly shook off the poisonous snake that had attached itself to his hand. One must ask, 'what purpose would religious snake handling have?' All of the gifts that were bestowed on the first century Christians had a practical purpose. The number one purpose was to evidence to the Jews that the Israelite nation was no longer the way to God, faith in Jesus Christ was.

As for Tongues, They Will Cease

Some may argue that the evidence does not give one any idea of when the gift of tongues was to end. However, they would be mistaken in this case. There are three lines of evidence that present the fact that the gift of tongues would die out shortly after the death of the last apostle, which was the apostle John, who died about 98-100 C.E. **First,** the gift of tongues was always passed on to the person, only by an apostle: either by laying his hands on this one, or at least being present. (Acts 2:4, 14, 17; 10:44-46; 19:6; see also Acts 8:14-18.) **Second,** 1 Corinthians 13:8 informed the Corinthian reader specifically that this gift would "cease." In short, the Greek word for cease [*pausontai*], means to 'peter out,' or 'to die out,' not to be brought to a halt. We will deal with *pausontai* more extensively in a moment. **Third,** both one and two are exactly what happened when we look at the history of this gift of tongues. M'Clintock and Strong's *Cyclopaedia* (Vol. VI, p. 320) says that it is "an uncontested statement that during the first hundred years after the death of the apostles we hear little or nothing of the working of miracles by the early Christians." Therefore, following their passing off the scene and after those who in that way had obtained the gift of tongues breathed their last breath; the gift of tongues should have died out with these ones. (Elwell, 2001, 1207-8) This analysis concurs with the intention of those gifts as acknowledged at Hebrews 2:2-4.

Daniel B. Wallace in his *Greek Grammar Beyond the Basics* helps us to better comprehend how we are to understand *pausontai* of 1 Corinthians 13:8:

> If the voice of the verb here is significant, then Paul is saying either that tongues will cut themselves off (direct middle) or, more likely, cease of their own

accord, i.e., 'die out' without an intervening agent (indirect middle). It may be significant with reference to prophecy and knowledge, Paul used a different verb ([katargeo]) and out it in the passive voice. In vv 9-10, the argument continues: 'for we *know* in part and we *prophecy* in part; but when the perfect comes, the partial shall be done away with [katargethesontai].' Here again, Paul uses the same passive verb he had used with prophecy and knowledge and he speaks of the verbal counterpart to the nominal 'prophecy' and 'knowledge.' Yet he does not speak about *tongues* being done away 'when the perfect comes.' The implication *may* be that tongues were to have 'died out' on their own *before* the perfect comes. (Wallace 1996, 422)

Speaking in Tongues and Today's Christianity

The gift of tongues "in the NT has three functions: to show the progress of the gift of the Spirit to the various people groups in the book of Acts in a salvation-history context, as a way of revealing the content of the NT revelation, and as a means of communicating cross-linguistically."[3] The apostle Paul made it abundantly clear that the interpretation must be clear and understood for the benefit of all, not the glorification of one. (1 Corinthians 14:26-33) Paul gave a warning: "So with yourselves, if with your tongue you utter speech that is not intelligible, how will anyone know what is said? For you will be speaking into the air." 1 Corinthians 14:9

It is true that many of the early Christians received this gift of tongues by way of Holy Spirit, which did *not* bring forth speech that was incomprehensible or untranslatable nonsense. In accord with Paul's advice, the Holy Spirit made available speech that brought about an outcome in the gospel being "preached in all creation under heaven."— Colossians 1:23.

The church has been attempting with great vigor, to fulfill, Jesus Christ's command of "the gospel must first be proclaimed to all nations." (Mark 13:10) The same as was the case in the first-century, all nations are required to take notice of the message of the ransom death, resurrection, and ascension of Christ. This is achievable for the reason that God's Word has now been translated into over 2,300 languages. The unchanged Spirit that instilled the first Christians to speak in tongues is now sustaining the immense and extraordinary commission of the present-day church. 2 Timothy 1:13

Final Thoughts

Certainly, no writer wishes to be arrogantly dogmatic about a belief, an understanding of Scripture that could be overturned or adjusted before his eyes, as he grows in knowledge and understanding. The evidence seems to say that the gift of tongues was given to some in the infant Christian congregation to establish it as the new way to God, to give witness to the mighty acts of God that include the ransom sacrifice of Christ, his resurrection, and ascension, and to communicate rapidly to those who spoke other languages.

These abilities were only established by the presence or lying on of hands by the apostles. This coincides with 1 Corinthians 13:8 and the history of these phenomena. Our Greek word for "cease" means that the gift of tongues was to 'die out' over time as the last of those who had received this gift passed off the scene of this earth. This is established by the historical fact that the second century saw just that being evidenced. Today, the Christian is moved by Spirit to speak with his heart and mind, defending and establishing the gospel, and destroying false doctrines, snatching some back from the fire. It is these things, which will give credence to the words of the modern-day Christian congregation: "God is really among you." 1 Corinthians 14:24, 25[64]

---

[64] Edward D. Andrews, *MIRACLES - DO THEY STILL HAPPEN TODAY? God Miraculously Saving People's Lives, Apparitions, Speaking In Tongues, Faith Healing* (Cambridge, OH: Christian Publishing House, 2015), 69-91.

CHAPTER 5 Error Gives Birth to Error: The New Apostolic Reformation

Despite all that we've learned so far, I know many Christians will still have a challenging time accepting that they need to stop listening to some of their favorite preachers and quickly! If you're still struggling with this, I'd encourage you to consider the following:

- *Is their theology biblical?*
- *Are their doctrines biblical?*
- *Do they teach correctly on God, Jesus and the Holy Spirit?*
- *Do they teach correctly regarding salvation?*
- *Do they teach what scripture says, without adding to it or forcing it to say that which it does not?*

If they're teaching Word of Faith, the answer is a resounding *no*, and we should also ask what these teachers have given birth to. What is their spiritual fruit? We are about to see how error begets error.

Today there is a growing and thriving movement, that has evolved from the same heresies that produced the Word of Faith Movement. They are commonly known as the New Apostolic Reformation, although by the time you read this, they may have changed their name. They have been known to evade labels so that when their adherents and supporters are accused of embracing their bizarre beliefs, they can pretend that they're not a part of it as they know how controversial it is.

The New Apostolic Reformation is a movement which proclaims that God is restoring to the church the offices of Apostles and Prophets, and that all believers should submit to their authority to establish the Kingdom of God on earth, and that this must take place before Jesus can return. And of course, these new apostles are all self-appointed, expecting us to believe that *God told them* they are apostles. To establish the Kingdom, they claim that under their leadership, the church must infiltrate and take dominion over all significant spheres of society and turn the world into a glorious Christian theocracy. Thus, the movement is also referred to as Dominionism or Kingdom Now Theology.

Before we go much deeper, let's address the fact that this ideology completely contradicts biblical prophecy. Scripture tells us there will be a great falling away from the truth, and that the world will become an increasingly wicked, evil and violent place, and that Jesus could return at any time. It should come as no surprise that these self-appointed "apostles" expect us to believe that they got their ideology via divine revelation.

Some of them even claim that they travel to heaven on a regular basis to get their assignments. If you thought that the Word of Faith movement was bad, be aware that the New Apostolic Reformation is Word of Faith on steroids, plus much, much more.

Like Word of Faith, the New Apostolic Reformation - or NAR - gladly borrows from New Age and occult practices, but much more blatantly. You will find eastern-style meditation techniques masked as *contemplative prayer*. *(And when you're told to empty your mind, and wait for God's voice, how do you know some deceiving spirit may not be speaking to you?)* You will find folks from a church called Bethel Redding cozying up to a movement called *Christalignment,* which even offers use of a *"Christianized"* Ouija Board, and Tarot Cards! *(Bethel's second in command, Kris Valloton has waffled on these accusations, posting on social media that Bethel has nothing to do with these things, and then turning around and defending them, then ultimately deleting the posts in question.)* You will find practitioners of what amounts to psychic readings and fortune telling labeled as *spiritual readings. (Bethel definitely promotes this!)*

You will also find folks practicing *Sozo* healing, which is particularly disconcerting. Sozo is the brainchild of Bethel pastors Bill and Benni Johnson and is decidedly unbiblical. Sozo is billed as a deliverance ministry that seeks to heal one from things in their past which may have allowed demonic influence to come upon them. The technique borrows directly from New Age and occult practices such as guided imagery. Some folks who been through it have given testimonies of how they became demonically oppressed because of the process. Some folks have described being encouraged to dig up memories of negative events, and then spirit-travel to the courts of heaven to have these memories erased. It is not biblical, and again, it borrows from the occult, which is something believers should never embrace. It should also be noted that Sozo steers people away from seeking their answers in scripture, and towards mystical, experience-driven encounters, which can potentially kick the doors of deception wide open.

You will also find people going to the graves of people like Aimee Semple McPherson, and Kathryn Kuhlman to *suck up their anointing.* Benny Hinn boasts of having done this many time. (The Bible calls this *necromancy* and an abomination.) Some call the practice *grave-sucking* or *grave soaking. (Bill Johnson denies that they do this, and yet is assembling a museum filled with relics belonging to dead "Christians" because their so-called anointing is still there to be claimed.)* You will be offered instructions about how to *spirit-travel* between realms. You may also hear reports of angel feathers and gold dust falling from the rafters, *(There is a testimony out there of a former Bethelite who admits she was told to put gold glitter in the ventilation system! And someone took some feathers to a lab, where they were determined to be ordinary bird feathers!)* gemstones appearing out of nowhere and rotten teeth suddenly receiving gold fillings. *(And don't you think that if the real Jesus were involved, He would just give them a brand new perfect tooth? Did he give paraplegics a golden crutch or did he heal them completely?)* Does this sound biblical? It doesn't because it's not. And let's repeat that the *appearance* of supernatural manifestations does not endorse false teaching; neither would the Holy Spirit of Almighty God manifest in a place where such blatantly unbiblical doctrines are taught.

These people claim the ability to impart all manner of Holy Spirit manifestations unto others, and - as we've discussed - one can reasonably ask if the spirit is indeed holy, when the manifestations take the form of people screaming as if on fire, twitching, jerking, making animal sounds, violently convulsing or giggling uncontrollably in fits of so-called *holy laughter.*

Hopefully, you can see some valid reasons to doubt that the NAR has any part in true, biblical Christianity, so let's take a closer look at the church most closely associated with it today, Bethel Church in Redding, California. We've mentioned Bethel's senior pastor, Bill Johnson, who propagates a whole host of heretical teachings, notably the *kenosis* doctrine. The *kenosis* doctrine teaches that Jesus abandoned His divinity during His incarnation; that He lived his earthly life as just an ordinary man. We have already seen this belief in the teachings of folks like Kenneth Copeland and Creflo Dollar. *(Biblically, it is correct to say that Jesus emptied Himself of the display of certain divine attributes, although He could have chosen to use and display them at any time. For example, He could have supernaturally removed Himself from the cross, but He chose not to, as that was not part of God's plan.)* Like them, Johnson asserts that if Jesus could perform spectacular miracles as an ordinary man in right relationship with God, there is no reason why we cannot heal paraplegics and raise the dead. Of course, neither Bill Johnson nor anyone from Bethel has succeeded at such feats so far. At the risk of redundancy, let's remember that Jesus did indeed claim to be God, accepted worship as God, and did things only God could do. Also, if Jesus was just a man, He would have had a sin nature, and *would have sinned* no matter how strong His relationship with The Father was; therefore, His death on the cross would not have been an acceptable sacrifice for the sins of mankind. God required a *spotless lamb*. All other heresies aside, this doctrine that Jesus was just an ordinary man on earth is enough by itself to brand those teaching it as heretics.

As might be expected of a NARpostle, Johnson's vision is that of a new "*Elijah generation"* spurring a great end times revival, with signs and wonders more spectacular than those of Jesus and the Apostles. They defend this notion by a gross misapplication of John 14:12...

John 14:12 Updated American Standard Version (UASV)

¹² Truly, truly, I say to you, the one trusting in me, the works that I do, he will do also; and greater works than these he will do; because I go to the Father.

Most scholars that I've studied say that Jesus, in this passage, was referring to the fact that after His ascension, His disciples would be spreading the gospel around the world and seeing eternal souls become born again. The salvation of a reprobate sinner is an infinitely greater work than any other miracle. And remember, miracles were never an end unto themselves; they were performed to validate the messengers. The NAR, however implies that miracles, signs and wonders will take center stage in their great end times revival, in which they don't really preach the true gospel, but basically just tell people that God loves them. That, of course is a false gospel with no power to save.

> **14:12.** This is one of the most interesting verses in the Bible. Interpreters have pondered what Jesus meant by telling his disciples that they would do greater things than he, the Son of God, had done. But perhaps the best way to understand the verse is to take it literally, exactly as Jesus said it. Jesus' earthly ministry was limited in time and space. He served the Father for three and one-half years and never outside the boundaries of Palestine. The disciples, on the other hand, as Acts clearly attests, carried out ministry that was greater geographically, in terms of numbers of people reached and long-lasting effect.
>
> We find a leadership principle here as well. All parents should be able to say to their children; all pastors should be able to say to their staffs; all leaders should be able to say to their followers: "You have the potential to do greater things than I have done." To empower and develop followers whose ministry exceeds the impact of their mentors is to follow the model of Jesus.[65]

And of course, these great signs and wonders are what will attract people to this false gospel and this delusion that they're going to establish the very Kingdom of God on earth. Johnson's vision has absolutely zero

---

[65] Kenneth O. Gangel, *John*, vol. 4, Holman New Testament Commentary (Nashville, TN: Broadman & Holman Publishers, 2000), 266–267.

biblical support, but his deluded followers are convinced that these new *apostles* have knowledge that trumps that dusty old Bible.

This denial of Jesus' divinity, the denial of the sovereignty of God, the elevation of man to a divine, miracle-working mini-God; these are all standard fare for the NAR, just like WOF. It is unbiblical, and it is just plain wrong. And like other WOF / NAR teachers, Johnson also insists that Jesus had to be born again. Again, the Jesus of scripture never had a sin nature, never suffered in hell, and certainly had no need of being born again.

Johnson also denies the sole authority of scripture, claiming that we should be open to new revelations all the time. In one of his most disturbing quotes, he says,

"*It's difficult to expect the same fruit of the early church when we value a book they didn't have more than the Holy Spirit they did have. It's not Father, Son and Holy Bible.*"

This dim view of Scripture is par for the course with these so-called new apostles. Think about how he's disrespecting God's Word here. Scripture tells us that Jesus *is* the Word made flesh. Therefore, scripture *is Jesus revealed in words.* To say that the Bible is less important than the Holy Spirit is an insult to the Holy Spirit, who reveals Himself to us in its very words! Furthermore, his statement implies that the Holy Spirit is going to teach us things *contrary* to scripture! This is heresy, plain and simple. In other words, to say that the early church did not have the Bible is disingenuous at best; they had the *Author of it!*

This all leads us to discuss a growing phenomenon in the modern church, which is often lamented (and rightly so) as the *Bethelization of Christianity.* What's being taught at Bethel and other NAR churches is becoming extremely popular in churches around the world, simply because it appeals to the flesh and the ego. Who wouldn't want to hear that God wants you healthy and rich, plus the fact that you're a divine being with the power to prophesy, heal the sick, raise the dead, and even be a part of the elite generation that ushers in the Kingdom of God on earth? And you won't hear the whole gospel being preached (they like to leave out that annoying stuff about sin and repentance); you'll just hear that God loves you, and you can walk in an amazing and abundant supernatural lifestyle. It's not the truth.

Bill Johnson not only claims to be an apostle, but he and others in the NAR claim to have an even greater anointing than the biblical Apostles and again, they are about to do even greater signs and wonders than those recorded in scripture. Of course, they know this by divine revelation. There are some in the movement who even claim to have gone to heaven, and learned straight from Peter, Paul, and company that the original Apostles are *jealous* of them! And we are to believe this just because *they* say so!

One event that especially highlights all that is wrong with the NAR is something that happened when their most elite leaders gathered to commission a new *Super Apostle*. What took place on June 23, 2008, is something the NAR folks would like swept under the rug and never mentioned again. Several of the most prominent self-proclaimed apostles, including Bill Johnson along with self-proclaimed prophets, C. Peter Wagner and Rick Joyner assembled in Lakeland, Florida to officially "commission" a man by the name of Todd Bentley as a member of their apostolic elite.

Their prophetic gifting had revealed that Bentley was a mighty man of God. They prophesied over him that his favor, authority, power and influence would increase. In addition, a new surge of supernatural power would flow through his ministry, as he helped establish the governance of the Kingdom.

Within two months of said commissioning, it appeared that these prophets were either terribly wrong or had misheard the Lord about this wonderful and mighty *man of God*. A so-called revival being led by Bentley, fell apart as he was exposed for having an affair and abandoning his wife and children. Outside investigations into his claims of healings and even raising the dead showed nothing but fraud. On top of that, he was conducting his services drunk, all the while boasting of his alleged miracles and his frequent contact with an angel named Emma.

You might think that if these modern-day apostles and prophets had any integrity, they would admit they'd been wrong and apologized. But no; Bentley was a NAR celebrity and a big draw at their events. He brought in a lot of tithes and offerings, so they found it expedient to restore him as quickly as possible - and they did so with great fanfare. Lest you think I'm being too judgmental here, let me explain. I certainly know that we all sin, and God will forgive the truly repentant. But Bentley never appeared very sorry, never underwent any significant period of restorative counseling, never attempted to reconcile with his wife, and wasted no time marrying his mistress in the midst of all this.

To this day Bentley continues as a golden child amongst the NAR inner circle, holding huge meetings around the world, promoting NAR heresies and gaining fame for antics such as kicking people in the face or punching them in the stomach to impart "healings." And he continues to make outrageous claims of raising the dead devoid of believable witnesses or documentation. Some of his recent dead-raising claims were purported to have taken place in hospitals, but verifications or medical records are always conveniently absent.

The nature of what goes on at places like Bethel is so bizarre, it amazes me that people can't see through it. But the Bible does say that people who follow false teachers will be under a "strong delusion," a fact that is easily observed. As we did earlier with Word of Faith, I'm not going to present a detailed section on every NAR teacher out there; they all espouse the same doctrines, but as we look further into the movement, we'll touch on some of the key players. In this age of the internet, it's very easy to see for yourself what goes on at NAR events, and it's rather shocking.

There's a video out there of a self-proclaimed "prophetess," Heidi Baker, rolling around on a platform, looking so intoxicated that she can't fulfill her obligation to speak, and at times she asks if someone else wants to take the mic. When she does speak it's basically, "shaka bobba.... whoa.... whoa.... shaka bobba...." In another instance, she lays hands on a young man, who then screams in pain as if he'd been thrown into a fire. Ms. Baker casually walks away while the young man thrashes on the floor, still screaming in agony. Does this sound like the work of the Holy Spirit? Certainly not to me. And all the while these things are taking place, you see Bill Johnson strolling in the background like it's just another day at the office. If you think you could stomach watching this for yourself, just google, *Heidi Baker imparts demons*; you'll find this video and others just as bad.

The Song of Seduction

One way places like Bethel are seducing people - especially young people - to their counterfeit gospel is with their extremely popular worship music. Just check out the worship songs that your own church might be using, and you may see that they are copyrighted to *Bethel Music*. This poses a conundrum as most churches don't want to be told what music they should use. And to be fair, most of the lyrics being sung don't reveal anything blatantly false; most of the songs appear doctrinally sound, but here is the problem: Once people become attracted to Bethel Music, they may learn that it comes from a church called Bethel, and they'll want to see what that's all about. If the music is so good, the church must be something special as well. Starting to see the problem? A casual look at Bethel might not reveal their heresy right up front. Like most false teachers, they mix their heresies with a lot of legit-sounding Christian terminology, even a pinch -and not much more - of actual truth. Before you know it, people - especially impressionable youth, or those not well grounded in scripture - are caught up in an experience-driven spirituality that downplays scripture and encourages folks to *go off the map*; Bill Johnson's smooth term for embracing teachings that go beyond what scripture instructs. *(Paul warned Timothy to watch his life and his doctrine carefully, and to not go beyond what is written)* It doesn't take long before people get swept away in a sea of emotionalism rather than being fed the Word of God, chasing after the next holy ghost high...and the next....and the next, all the while being fed a toxic brew of spiritual poison.

At the risk of redundancy, I should note that Hillsong is just as bad. They draw people in with their popular music, but the leaders of Hillsong Church (and its satellite churches) promote unadulterated Word of Faith and Prosperity falsehoods.

The siren song of Bethel is bringing in droves of people courtesy of their worship band, Jesus Culture. Jesus Culture produces a lot of very popular music, attracting a great many people to them. The most well-known and popular member of Jesus Culture is vocalist Kim Walker Smith. I've heard her sing in person; she has a beautiful voice. It's a shame that she uses that voice to lure people towards the apostasy that is Bethel. Also, worth noting is her public testimony of having been transported to heaven for an encounter with Jesus. Some folks will say, how can you dispute that? How can you know it didn't happen? I would say her testimony is a perfect example of the deceptive visions and revelations so prevalent in the NAR. Let's look at her statement, and see if it bears any resemblance to some biblical descriptions of the glorious risen and ascended Christ...

Revelation 1:12-17 Updated American Standard Version (UASV)

[12] Then I turned to see the voice that was speaking with me. And having turned I saw seven golden lampstands; [13] and in the middle of the lampstands I saw one like a son of man, clothed in a robe reaching to the feet, and girded across his chest with a golden sash. [14] his head and his hair were white like white wool, like snow; and his eyes were like a flame of fire.[15] his feet were like burnished bronze, when it has been made to glow in a furnace, and his voice was like the sound of many waters. [16] In his right hand He held seven stars, and out of his mouth came a sharp two-edged sword; and his face was like the sun shining in its strength.

[17] When I saw him, I fell at his feet like a dead man. And He placed his right hand on me, saying, "Do not be afraid; I am the first and the last,

Does this passage not indicate that an encounter with the ascended Christ is not something one would describe casually?

> **1:12–16.** Many have noted the oddity of John's saying that he **turned around to see the voice**, since voices are heard not seen. Obviously, he means that he turned to see who was speaking—the response everyone would have to such a sound. In this case, and in all

the similar ones throughout Revelation, John's strange expressions are perfectly understandable. Each of the **seven golden lampstands** was probably a seven-branched candelabrum, such as the one placed in the Israelite tabernacle of the Old Testament (Exod. 25:36–40). In Zechariah 4:2, such a lampstand represented Israel; now each lampstand represents one of the Christian churches, God's new people (v. 20). Just as lampstands bring physical light to the darkness, so Christ's churches bring moral light to a wicked world (Matt. 5:14).

The exalted Jesus appeared in splendid form. Johns vision of Jesus is similar to, but clearly outstrips Daniel's vision of a revealing angel (Dan. 10:5–6). The Gospels nowhere describe the physical appearance of Jesus; hundreds of artists have used their imagination to fill in the gap. The current description is symbolic, not literal, for the picture becomes bizarre if, say, the sword coming from his mouth is literal. Note also the number of times *like* is used. No artist could paint what John described. The meaning of these symbols is not very difficult, as the following discussion makes clear. Our discussion is somewhat subjective, as shown by opinions of other commentators, but our suggestions do have good historical support.

Location. John sees Jesus **among the lampstands**. The one who "loves us and freed us from our sins" (v. 5) is first presented in Revelation not enthroned in heaven or fighting evil but present with and caring for his people. Suffering Christians throughout the ages have taken comfort in Jesus' presence with them.

Shape. Jesus is **someone "like a son of man."** At the least, this identities Jesus as maintaining his essential humanity even in his exalted state. John's Gospel records that Jesus often called himself "Son of man," which makes unmistakable that this figure is the same Jesus that John had followed as a disciple decades earlier. It also strengthens the identity between Jesus and the splendid figure of Daniel 7:13. The same Jesus that once lived and walked in Galilee is now described as glorious and powerful beyond imagination

Clothing. The **robe reaching down to his feet and with a golden sash around his chest** links him in appearance with the high priest of Israel (Exod. 39:2–4). We have already seen Jesus described in priest-like terms in this chapter. This clothing symbolizes his ongoing work of representing his people before his Father.

Hair. The hair appeared **like wool, as white as snow**. In the ancient world, white hair symbolized the respect due to the aged for the wisdom of their advanced years (Prov. 16:31). This part of the picture points to Jesus' wisdom. In traditional theological language, the "omniscience" of the exalted Jesus may be suggested. He knows what is best for his people, even when they are suffering.

Eyes. The eyes of Jesus appeared **like blazing fire.** This may mean that he sees everything there is to see (Ps. 139). In theological terms, this may refer to the "omnipresence" of Jesus. He sees the evil of this world; he sees his people in their distress; one day he will respond with righteous fury.

Feet. The feet are **like bronze glowing in a furnace.** The introduction to one of the great psalms about the coming Messiah announces, "The lord says to my Lord: Sit at my right hand until I make your enemies a footstool for your feet" (Ps. 110:1). The picture is of a powerful king who has so subdued his enemies that they are nothing more than the king's footstool. Some ancient kings symbolized their victories by literally placing their feet on the necks of defeated enemies. These powerful feet of Jesus point to his ultimate triumph over all the forces of evil, natural and supernatural alike. If his hair symbolizes "omniscience" and his eyes "omnipresence," then the feet may represent "omnipotence."

Voice. In verse 10, Jesus' voice was compared to a trumpet that could not be ignored. Now his voice is compared to **the sound of rushing waters,** which also cannot be ignored. On Patmos, John likely could never get away from the insistent sound of the breakers coming off the Mediterranean Sea. The voice of Jesus is the Word of God that must be constantly heard and obeyed (vv. 2, 9).

Hands. In the right hand of Jesus, John saw **seven stars.** In verse 20 the stars are explained as the *angels* of the seven churches. Some interpreters see these as meaning a guardian angel for each congregation, an idea found nowhere else in the New Testament (although Matt. 18:10 affirms that individuals have guardian angels). Other interpreters see these in the sense of human *messengers,* that is, those who were to convey the message of Revelation safely to their respective churches (see 2:1, 8, 12). These would almost certainly have been the pastors of the churches. Although I prefer this second interpretation, I believe John's main point is that Jesus sovereignly **held** these persons in his protection and care.

weapon. The strangest part of this picture is that **out of his mouth came a sharp double-edged sword.** The sword described is a long sword for battle rather than a dagger. According to Revelation 19:15, "Out of his mouth comes a sharp sword with which to strike down the nations." The sword stands for Jesus' power to judge and conquer his enemies, thus protecting his people.

Face. The element of the vision John noted last, perhaps because it was the most important, was Jesus' face: **like the sun shining in all its brilliance.** Here John can only mean the glory of full deity. In Matthew 17:2, Jesus' face "shone like the sun" at his Transfiguration. The Jesus that John, saw both on the Mount of Transfiguration and on the island of Patmos, is none other than Almighty God.

1:17–18. John made the only right response that humans can make to the direct appearance of God: **I fell at his feet as though dead.** When God visibly manifests himself, worship must follow, as biblical testimony from Moses onward makes clear (Exod. 3:6). Worship was followed by blessing. The powerful right hand that had held the seven stars now blesses John. The commanding voice that had thundered like a trumpet and like many waters now speaks comfort—comfort based on Jesus' mighty power.

His power over time. The words **Do not be afraid** are Jesus' immediate words of blessing to calm John's terror. He then tells why he has a right to bless: **I am the First and Last.** This is similar in wording to "Alpha and Omega" (v. 8). Jesus is master from before the beginning of time until after the end of time and through all eternity.

His power over life. Because he is **the Living One**, he is the Creator and sustainer of all life. This is the only time this designation is given to Jesus in the New Testament. John has, however, called him "living water" (John 4:10–11) and "living bread" (6:51). Jesus lives through the living Father, and in like manner believers live through Jesus (John 6:57). Those living and believing in Jesus shall never die (John 11:26). Hebrews speaks of the living Word (4:12) and of Jesus living to make intercession for us (7:25). Jesus lives to pray for us just as he died to save us. Because he has unending life, he has the power to extend eternal life to all who trust in him.

His power over sin. He is the one who **was dead ... and alive forever**, an obvious reference to Jesus' historical victory over sin and death. This aspect of Jesus' work on behalf of his people is further emphasized in chapter 5 with the portrait of the Lamb who was slaughtered.

His power over death. **Keys** are for opening or locking doors. **Death and Hades**—twin monsters—are limited in their power by the keyholder. As the final Judge, Jesus is able to "open the doors of death" and judge all those who have died. He also has the power to send into eternal death ("the lake of fire") those whose names are not recorded in

> the Book of Life. The portrait of the last judgment in Revelation 20 expands this theme, especially verses 14–15.[66]

Acts 9:3-6 Updated American Standard Version (UASV)

³ Now as he was traveling and nearing Damascus, suddenly a light from heaven flashed around him. ⁴ And falling to the ground he heard a voice saying to him, "Saul, Saul, why are you persecuting me?" ⁵ And he said, "Who are you, Lord?" And he said, "I am Jesus, whom you are persecuting. ⁶ But get up and enter into the city, and it will be told to you what you must do."

Here again we see an encounter with the risen and ascended Christ being described as awe-inspiring to say the least.

> **9:3–4.** Saul had nearly completed the six-day journey as he approached Damascus, 175 miles northeast of Jerusalem, the second oldest city in the world still in existence (Tarsus is the oldest). Now God turned a mission of hate into a message from heaven. Saul saw a light and heard a voice from heaven; for a devout Jew, this would always mean a word from God.
>
> This was no ordinary light. Remember it shone at midday (22:6). Saul describes it as **a light from heaven, brighter than the sun** (26:13). The various accounts of this event suggest that only Saul understood the message from heaven although those with him heard the sound. The Greek word for "voice" (*phone*) supports that idea since it means both sound and specific articulated speech. The question from heaven must have stunned Saul into disbelief. Persecuting God? He was doing exactly the reverse—persecuting those who blasphemed God.
>
> **9:5–6.** The Greek *kyrios* could mean "sir." Some have suggested that Saul used that innocuous and polite form of address. More likely (in view of light and sound coming down from above), he meant to say, "Lord" in a worshipful way. He could never have prepared himself for the answer to his question: **I am Jesus, whom you are persecuting.** Before he could recover from that shock he received new orders to **go into the city**, the first of many commands from Christ this man would obey. In Saul's view, one of the worst aspects of Christian blasphemy had been their claim that Jesus of Nazareth was alive; now he must face this reality.
>
> The Lord imparted to his newly-chosen one a new faith, a new interpretation of the Old Testament, a new perspective on divine

---

[66] Kendell H. Easley, *Revelation*, vol. 12, Holman New Testament Commentary (Nashville, TN: Broadman & Holman Publishers, 1998), 18–20.

> redemption, a new eschatology, a new identification with followers of the Way, and a new mission for his life. To be sure, all of that would unfold in the weeks, months, and years ahead, but it began precisely at this moment on the Damascus Road.[67]

Testimony of Kim Walker Smith, edited for conciseness -

"...So, I had this encounter, all the sudden I see Jesus standing in front of me and He's reaching for me like this (gestures)—like He wants me to come to Him.... And Jesus (laughs) is completely irresistible...

Anyways, (pause) so, irresistible, I go to Jesus, I fall in His arms. And as I'm laying in His arms, I'm still feeling kind of afraid to really even look at Him. All the sudden this thought comes into my mind, and I know this is not my thought. I would never, ever, ever in a million, trillion years think this; and I think, "I need to ask Him two questions." I need to ask Him, "How much do You love me; and what were You thinking when You created me?" .... And all the sudden, Jesus...starts stretching out his arms, k. They're each going out each way; and it looked like Stretch Armstrong.

So, Jesus, k, His arms are like stretching out forever and ever, and I'm looking and looking, and I can't see the ends. I can't see where it's ending; and he starts laughing, and he goes, "I love you this much ha, ha, ha, ha, ha!" And He's laughing hysterically. (audience laughs) And then, I start laughing. I'm cracking up. I'm—I'm suddenly like—I'm—I'm becoming like so full of joy; and I'm just like, "What?! You love me that much?!" I can't even see the ends—it's going on forever and ever and ever. Oh, my goodness, I can't— "You love me that much?"

...And again, He was completely irresistible. And I fall on the floor; I start sobbing—like I do in His presence—and I finally say to Him, "Jesus, what were You thinking when You created me?" And suddenly; I'm standing with Jesus. And just in front of me is God the Father and He's got a table in front of Him; and He reaches into His heart and He rips this chunk off of His heart, and He throws it on the table.

And it's suddenly, like, clay or Play-Doh. And He starts molding it and shaping it, and I'm like, "Jesus, (pointing) what is He doing? Wh—What's He making? What is He making?" And all of the sudden I see—He makes me! I'm there—on the table. And He reaches over; and He grabs this box and brings it over, and He sets me inside the box. And, you know those little jewelry boxes that little girls have; where you open it up and it plays music, and the little ballerina, like, twirls? Hello? Do you know what I'm

---

[67] Kenneth O. Gangel, *Acts*, vol. 5, Holman New Testament Commentary (Nashville, TN: Broadman & Holman Publishers, 1998), 139.

talking about? (laughs) No? Do they not make those anymore? (audience laughs)

My goodness. I'm not old, k? (audience laughs) And um, it was a box like that. And He shuts the box; and He gets in front of it. (crouches) And He's like really excited. Kinda' looks around, and He opens the box, real fast like that! (motions upward) And when He does, inside, I start twirling, and dancing, and singing to Him and worshipping Him. And He goes, "Woohoo! Woooo!" (acts like running around) He, like, runs around—He runs around and He comes back, and He closes the box, And He's like (looks side to side grinning as audience laughs and then motions upward). And He throws it open again and He's like, "Woohoo!" And He starts running around in circles again, and He comes back over, and He closes it again.

So, the *"Jesus"* Kim Walker Smith sees, sounds so much like the Jesus described in Revelation and Acts, doesn't he? Biblical revelations of the real Jesus are both awe-inspiring, and majestic to the point of terrifying. But the *"Jesus"* described by Kim resembles Stretch Armstrong and runs around hysterically laughing and shouting, *"Whoo! Hoo!"*

Anyone besides me seeing a problem with this? Just doing the obvious math, I highly doubt that Kim had a genuine encounter with the real Jesus. Furthermore, if she had seen the real Jesus, I'm pretty sure he would have told her to get out of that hotbed of heresy known as Bethel. This account of her heavenly visit is typical of the false encounters reported by so many people associated with Bethel and the NAR in general. Jesse Duplantis, another WOF / NAR celebrity describes his frequent trips to heaven via golden cable cars where he encounters and comforts a sometimes-sad Jesus. In one account, he asked Jesus what's wrong and Jesus told him, *"I need ya, son!"* (And speaking of Jesse Duplantis and his preferred modes of travel, he is also infamous for a program he did with Kenneth Copeland, where they defended their need for multi-million-dollar private jets, claiming that if they flew on ordinary airlines they might be exposed to demonically possessed passengers, and how could they possibly prepare sermons under such conditions? Personally, I've heard some good preachers do an excellent job after flying coach.*

Sid Roth

For other accounts of dubious meetings with Jesus, one can always tune into *It's Supernatural with Sid Roth.* This program is a staple on TBN, Daystar and other religious networks. Roth has a reputation for hosting folks with all kinds of tales of trips to heaven, and other experience-driven spirituality. One recent guest told Sid about his guided tour - by Jesus

Himself, of course - through heaven's spare body parts storeroom, as well as Jesus telling him that the book of John was missing its concluding chapter, which would soon be revealed. *(I had also heard Billy Burke explain that all the new stomachs, new kidneys, etc. were in a storehouse up in heaven and if someone needed one, we just have to call it down by faith. Seriously - you can't make this stuff up!)* How is it that the people caught up in this nonsense don't realize how these heavenly visits don't line up with scripture at all?

Remember how Paul spoke of his vision of heaven?

2 Corinthians 12:2-4 Updated American Standard Version (UASV)

² I know a man in Christ who fourteen years ago, whether in the body I do not know, or out of the body I do not know, God knows, such a man was caught up to the third heaven. ³ And I know how such a man, whether in the body or apart from the body I do not know, God knows; ⁴ was caught up into Paradise and heard unspeakable words, which a man is not permitted to speak.

CPH Note: This text comes immediately after verses in which Paul defended his apostleship. Considering that the Bible does not mention any other person who had such an experience as this and because it is Paul who tells us of it, it is very likely Paul had this vision. Some scholars have attempted to link Paul's reference to the third heaven to the early rabbinic belief that there were stages of heaven, as much as "seven heavens." Such a view has no support in the Scriptures. The heavens are not referred to specifically as if divided into stages or levels, but, rather, the context has to be relied upon to resolve whether the reference is to the heavens within earth's atmosphere where the birds fly, the heavens of the universe, or the spiritual heavens, or even something else. Thus, it seems that the reference to "the third heaven" is a reference to the superlative degree of the rapture in which the vision took place.

Paul is speaking of himself in the third person here. What he saw and heard was so awesome, so awe-inspiring that he could only say it was beyond human words. However, these modern visionaries speak of trips to heaven as casually as they would a trip to the beach.

Let's also consider the following scripture...

1 Corinthians 2:9 Updated American Standard Version (UASV)

⁹ But, as it is written,

"What no eye has seen, nor ear heard,
  nor the heart of man imagined,
all that God has prepared for those who love him."

This verse should lead one to believe that trips to heaven are not commonplace, if allowed at all!

It appears that a true vision of heaven and the risen Christ looks very different than what's being described by the NAR crowd. It also doesn't take much research to find that many of these alleged descriptions of heaven contradict each other. And again, any encounter with the real Jesus would have one running from all these false teachers as fast as possible!

The Supremacy of "Experience"

One thing you may have noticed by now with the NAR and WOF movements, is this tendency to elevate experiences and emotions to a significance higher than scripture. When people are questioned about their involvement in these things, they will often say, *"But I know what I experienced!"* Experiences *can* be valid, but if they lead one to believe things that scripture doesn't support, be very cautious. This is just as dangerous as seeking extra-biblical revelations, rather than being content with the revelation already given in scripture. Many a road to deception is paved with thoughts like, *I know what the Bible says but I want more....* God's revelation is complete in Christ and His Word, and scripture concludes with some stern warnings to anyone who would add to it...

Revelation 22:18 Updated American Standard Version (UASV)

[18] I testify to everyone who hears the words of the prophecy of this book: if anyone adds to them, God will add to him the plagues which are written in this book;

Scripture is complete. God does not want anyone to presume that they can add to it!

The Sufficiency of Scripture

As I'm taking a rather skeptical view of extra-biblical revelations, let's consider why we should stick to *sola scriptura - or scripture alone.* Consider Paul's second letter to Timothy...

2 Timothy 3:15-17 Updated American Standard Version (UASV)

[15] and that from infancy[68] you have known the sacred writings, which are able to make you wise for salvation through trust[69] in Christ Jesus. [16] All

---

[68] *Brephos* is the period of time when one is very young - childhood (probably implying a time when a child is still nursing), infancy.

[69] *Pisteuo* is "to believe to the extent of complete trust and reliance - 'to believe in, to have faith in, to trust, faith, trust

Scripture is inspired by God and profitable for teaching, for reproof, for correction, for training in righteousness; [17] so that the man of God may be fully competent. Equipped for every good work. *

Notice how Paul says here that Scripture is sufficient to make the man (or woman) of God perfectly equipped for every good work.

But this is not the only verse that speaks of the sufficiency of scripture.

Psalm 19:7 Updated American Standard Version (UASV)

[7] The law of Jehovah is perfect,
   restoring the soul;
the testimony of Jehovah is sure,
   making wise the simple.

Here, David is rejoicing that Scripture is perfect, despite the fact that the complete written Word had not yet been compiled. This does not mean that David would have foreknown that one day there would be a total of sixty-six book that completed the Bible. Perfect (Heb. tamim), meaning whole, complete, sufficient, lacking nothing, or comprehensive, reviving the soul, means that every verse of scripture is sufficient for its intended purpose. Each book of the Bible as it was penned under inspiration by human authors who were moved along by Holy Spirit was and is whole, complete, sufficient, lacking nothing, or comprehensive, reviving the soul.

And for those who might not find these verses convincing, let's think back to the Lord's strong warning at the end of Scripture's final book, Revelation *not to add to its words.*

19:7. Suddenly shifting focus, David gave attention to the glory of God revealed in his Word. He gave six descriptions of the sufficiency of God's written Word (vv. 7–9) which goes far beyond what natural revelation does. While the sun and the skies above reveal the existence and infinite power of God, Scripture reveals the only way to know God personally. **The law of the LORD is perfect** (Heb. *tamim*), meaning whole, complete, sufficient, lacking nothing, or comprehensive, reviving the soul. It is so perfect that it can convert, transform, and refresh the entire inner person.

The statutes of the LORD are trustworthy, meaning they are neither unstable nor fallible but unwavering and immovable. Not like shifting sands, God's commands cause a person to stand firm while **making wise the simple.** The Hebrew word for simple comes from a root meaning "an open door" or one who is gullible to false teaching, failing to shut

> his mind to error. Only *Scripture* can make a person **wise**, or skillful, in the issues of daily living.[70]

There simply is no need for new revelations. Scripture is God's complete revelation to us. Everything we need to know is already there. The canon is closed. But as we've seen, the folks in the WOF & NAR movements think they know better than scripture; thus, they can't wait for their next chance to *go off the map.*

A Look at the "Prophets"

One of the most prominent of the new self-appointed "prophets" is Rick Joyner, head of Morningstar Ministries. He proclaims all the standard Dominionist teachings:

"In the near future the church will not be looking back at the first century church with envy because of the great exploits of those days, but all will be saying that He certainly did save His best wine for last. The most glorious times in all of history have now come upon us. You who have dreamed of one day being able to talk with Peter, John and Paul are going to be surprised to find that they have all been waiting to talk to you! You have been chosen to see the harvest, the fruit of the seed that they were planting." - Rick Joyner

This all sounds very nice but it's blatantly unbiblical. He goes on to parrot the NAR party line that we are about to see signs and wonders far more spectacular than the Biblical ones, and that believers will interact with and even command angels in an unprecedented way. Once again, the prophecies of Joyner and his fellow NAR elite are totally lacking in biblical support. His only remotely biblical assertion is the one regarding an increase in the miraculous, and the only way that lines up with scripture is the fact that Satan will deceive with great signs and wonders.

Not surprisingly, Joyner is no fan of discernment ministries. He says the following:

"The more we focus on what is wrong, or the practices of the evil one, the more we, ourselves, will be changed into the nature of what we are seeing."

So basically, he's saying that examining false teachings will lead us to embrace the very thing we're investigating. Either that, or he doesn't want us to see how unbiblical his teachings and prophecies are. Among his teachings is the idea that there is no rapture. *(I know that Christians hold*

---

[70] Lawson, Steven. Holman Old Testament Commentary - Psalms: 11 (pp. 100-101). B&H Publishing Group.

to differing beliefs as to <u>when</u> the rapture will occur, but it's blatantly unbiblical to deny it altogether. Yes, there are believers who claim the rapture is based on a faulty interpretation of scripture - which I disagree with, but that is a whole other discussion. What does scripture mean when it says we shall all be caught up together with Him in the air?) Of course; the idea that Jesus will take his saints away from the earth before a period of great tribulation, flies in the face of the NAR doctrine that believers are about to spark a great revival and usher in the Kingdom of God. What can we say? The first notion is biblical; the second is not. Like other NAR leaders, his core teachings have zero scriptural support

Another of the NAR elite is "*prophet*," Lance Wallnau, known especially for promoting The *Seven Mountain Mandate*. This mandate is the idea is that Christians must take over the seven major spheres or mountains of societal influence, these being: *family, government, media, arts & entertainment, business, education and the church.*

It is especially telling what the NAR teaches about taking over the church. Aren't Christians already leading the (true) church? According to folks like Wallnau and Joyner, all churches must submit to the authority of the NAR - and its various apostles - or risk being left out of the Kingdom of God altogether. Chapter and verse? Where does scripture tells us that in the last days, believers must submit to this *new breed* of prophets? There is no biblical support for this fantasy, only the NAR's expectation that we should believe their claims of divine revelation. Personally, I do not believe for a second that God has revealed any of these things which contradict His Word!

There are many other false prophets gaining fame and fortune within the NAR. Joyner and Wallnau are but two representative examples, but it should be clear that the movement is rife with deception. We aren't going to study every false prophet in the movement but here are some names to beware of; they all teach the same things: Kris Valloton (second in command at Bethel), Mike Bickle, Jim Bakker *(who banks on us going through the Tribulation by hawking freeze-dried survival food)*, Cindy Jacobs, Jennifer Leclaire (whom we can thank for enlightening us that there's a *sneaky squid spirit* to watch out for), James Goll, and many more.

The NAR uses a lot of buzzwords, which they employ in ways that sound biblical on the surface, but they're usually a red flag for heresy. Watch for terms like *shifting atmospheres, breakthrough, divine destiny, supernatural assignments, prophetic art, waking up angels, in the heavenlies (often used when they speak of their frequent flier miles to heaven), alignment, vision casting, etc.* In NAR terminology these terms are used to promote the idea that God is doing a *new thing*, shifting the atmosphere towards revival, as NAR generals receive their supernatural assignments whilst traveling back and forth between realms. It all sounds very exciting, doesn't it? It's also totally unbiblical.

Another NAR doctrine that really excites their deluded followers is the *great supernatural wealth transfer.* Hot on the heels of the Prosperity Gospel, is the idea that very soon, we are going to see the wealth of the wicked magically transferred into the hands and bank accounts of believers. How, exactly this will happen is unknown but NAR proponents say it will somehow happen as believers take over the mountain of business, and slip into management roles. Sounds nice but has zero biblical support.

Unity at Any Cost

One of the most pervasive and unbiblical tenets of the Word of Faith and NAR movements is the idea that all segments of Christianity *(true and false)* should unite regardless of doctrinal differences. When they say that, of course they are including churches with no regard for the supremacy of scripture, such as Roman Catholicism. It is not my intent to bash Catholics, but it's a fact that the Roman church does not teach the gospel according to scripture. Catholicism teaches a work-based salvation, the worship of, and praying to the dead such as Mary and others, salvation contingent upon the sacraments of the church, confession of sins to the priesthood, etc. Martin Luther launched the Protestant Reformation five hundred years ago to get folks away from these man-made doctrines and back to the gospel as presented in scripture alone *(sola scriptura).* After all these years, we now see folks like Kenneth Copeland stating that Protestants should reunite with Roman Catholicism, and that the Pope is his *hero,* even stating that the Reformation was *demonic!* Many other WOF / NAR leaders are advocating likewise; rising star faith healer, Todd White (who practically hero worships Copeland) gushes about his dream that the Protestant church and the Catholic church are going to come back together. There are actually reports of charismatic congregations that have converted to Catholicism. Does any of this sound familiar? Scripture warns that in the end times there will be a great apostasy, (falling away from the truth) and that there will be a universal false church. I believe we see it forming before our very eyes. Mega-church pastor Rick Warren not only says that all Christians should submit to the Pope but even advocates unity with the evil known as Islam; something often referred to as Chrislam! Let's not forget scripture's admonition not to be unequally yoked, and to have nothing to do with the unfruitful works of darkness. And what else does scripture tell us about the apostate church? *"Come out of her, my people!"* True Christians should have nothing to do with this politically correct ecumenical movement.

What Does It All Mean?

So, what does all this mean for us? I once looked at the *(extreme)* charismatic movement and the televangelism scene (at least most of it) as a body of fellow believers who just had some misinformed doctrines, but is that a fair assessment? Given all that we've seen, nothing could be farther from the truth. Let's pause for a moment to consider scripture...

Galatians 1:8 Updated American Standard Version (UASV)

⁸ But even if we or an angel from heaven should proclaim to you a gospel contrary to[71] the one we preached to you, let him be accursed![72]

There should be absolutely no tolerance for any message contrary to the gospel proclaimed by the Apostles.

> **1:8.** A hypothetical case shows the seriousness of legalism's perversion of grace. Through hyperbole (a deliberate exaggeration for emphasis), Paul declares that anyone who preaches a mixture of grace and law is worthy of eternal condemnation. A teacher who requires others to obey the law as a requirement for salvation is leading others to a Christless eternity. Paul uses strong language because he is dealing with a life-or-death situation. You must choose: the gospel of grace Paul preached or the gospel of works the perverters preached.[73]

So where do we draw the line between doctrinal differences that are okay to differ on vs. what constitutes a *different gospel?* One main point is that any gospel that changes key doctrines on the nature of God, man, Christ, and what it means to be born again is a *different gospel* from that of scripture. Baptists hold to believer's baptism by immersion; Presbyterians believe in infant baptism by sprinkling. I believe in the former, but neither is something one's salvation is contingent upon. The same could be said of things like how often to observe communion, or one's understanding of predestination or eschatology. With that in mind, let's revisit some key doctrines of the Word of Faith and New Apostolic Reformation movement and ask ourselves if they are biblical.

The WOF / NAR movement teaches the following heresies:

---

[71] Or *other than*
[72] Gr *anathema*

[73] Max Anders, *Galatians-Colossians*, vol. 8, Holman New Testament Commentary (Nashville, TN: Broadman & Holman Publishers, 1999), 7.

We are little gods who are *sovereign* over the earth; our spoken words have the power to both *command and permit God - who is not sovereign - to act.*

Jesus came as *just an ordinary man* in right relationship to the father, and thus no miraculous thing He did is beyond what we, ourselves can do.

Jesus' death on the cross did three things; it *(partially) paid for our sins, it purchased our right to physical healing, and it paid for our claim to financial prosperity.*

Having only partially atoned for our sins on the cross, Jesus *had to suffer in hell and be born again.*

When we become born again, *we become just as much an incarnation of God as Jesus*, thus we regain our full divinity and godhood.

In our present day, God is restoring apostles and prophets to rule over the church, lead a great revival, take dominion over society, and usher in the glorious Kingdom of God before Jesus can return. In the words of Bill Johnson, they will *bring heaven to earth.*

I hope it is clear how this "gospel" is very different than that of scripture. Let's look at some significant differences.

The biblical God created us *in His image, not as reproductions of Himself.*

Our sin in the Garden separated us from God so He sent His Son *(fully man and fully God)* to live a sinless life and atone *completely* for our sins on the cross, from which He ascended *immediately* to the Father.

When we place our faith in Christ alone for our salvation, we become regenerated in our spirit, and are born again. We become renewed in Christ, but we do not become equal to Christ.

In the last days, there will be not a great revival, but a great *falling away* from the faith. A unified, but apostate church will rise to prominence, as the world becomes increasingly evil.

Christ will return to rapture[74] His church, although not all Christians agree as to when this will happen with regard to the tribulation. Ultimately, Christ will return with His church, and then and only then will the Kingdom of God be established.

By this point, it should be obvious that the gospel of the Word of Faith and NAR is a different gospel from that of scripture! I will admit that until

---

[74] CPH NOTE: Explaining the Rapture
https://christianpublishinghouse.co/2016/12/13/explaining-the-rapture/

rather recently, when I listened to certain people, I struggled to discern if they were talking about the real Jesus, and just had some horrible misunderstandings about Him, *(they may be immature, and not yet biblically literate)* or if they are truly embracing a *different Jesus. I am now convinced that Word of Faith & NAR teachers are proclaiming an utterly false gospel.* We should stick with teachings that have solid biblical support. Anything less is a slippery and *very* dangerous slope.

What about the Fruit?

Even with all the overwhelming evidence against certain popular false teachers, some folks will still stubbornly defend them, pointing to their *fruit* of good works. *But they've done so much good for people! People are coming to Jesus through them! Joyce Meyer provides clean water to third world countries! Heidi Baker helps orphans in Mozambique!* To which I would simply say, so what? Sounds harsh, but just as miracles do not validate false teachings, neither do charitable deeds. Catholics, Mormons and Jehovah's Witnesses do good works. So, do atheists - but I would never recommend their *teachings* to you. As for people coming to Jesus - once again - are they? Or are they unfortunately embracing a false, unbiblical Jesus; a *different gospel?* Satan will gladly help an old lady across the street if it furthers his agenda but he's still evil.

CHAPTER 6 Why Does God Allow False Teachers?

There's a quote from Pastor Paul Washer that's going viral around the internet:

"False teachers are God's judgment on people who don't want God, but in the name of religion plan on getting everything their carnal heart desires. That's why a Joel Osteen is raised up! Those people who sit under him are not victims of him, he is the JUDGMENT OF GOD UPON THEM BECAUSE THEY WANT EXACTLY WHAT HE WANTS AND IT'S NOT GOD!"

Wow, that's harsh, you might think! So, let's look to the Scriptures as we consider this and proceed from there...

2 Thessalonians 2:8-12 Updated American Standard Version (UASV)

⁸ Then the lawless one will be revealed, whom the Lord Jesus will do away with by the spirit of his mouth, and wipe out by the appearance[75] of his coming,[76] ⁹ namely, the one whose coming is in accordance with the activity of Satan, with all power and signs and false wonders, ¹⁰ and with every unrighteous deception[77] for those who are perishing, because they did not receive the love of the truth so as to be saved. ¹¹ For this reason God is sending upon them a powerful delusion[78] so that they will believe the lie, ¹² in order that they all may be judged because they did not believe the truth but took pleasure in unrighteousness.

God himself will send a deluding influence upon those who do not love the truth.

---

[75] **Appearing**: (Gr. *epiphaneia*) It literally means "a shining forth," which was used to refer to a divine being becoming visible to humans. *Epiphaneia* is used in the NT to refer to Jesus first coming to the earth and his second coming as well. – 2 Thess. 2:8; 1 Tim. 6:14; 2 Tim. 1:10; 4:1, 8.

[76] **Presence; Coming**: (Gr. *parousia*) The Greek word literally means," which is derived from *para*, meaning "with," and *ousia*, meaning "being." It denotes both an "arrival" and a consequent "presence with." Depending on the context, it can mean "presence," "arrival," "appearance," or "coming." In some contexts, this word is describing the presence of Jesus Christ in the last days, i.e., from his ascension in 33 C.E. up unto his second coming, with the emphasis being on his second coming, the end of the age of Satan's reign of terror over the earth. We do not know the day nor the hours of this second coming. (Matt 24:36) It covers a marked period of time with the focus on the end of that period. – Matt. 24:3, 27, 37, 39; 1 Cor. 15:23; 16:17; 2 Cor. 7:6-7; 10:10; Php 1:26; 2:12; 1 Thess. 2:19; 3:13; 4:15; 5:2.

[77] Lit *seduction*

[78] Or *a deluding influence*; Lit *an operation of deceit*

Most commentaries would say that this passage is referring to the coming of the Antichrist, so why would Washer apply it to a theological lightweight like Joel Osteen? Osteen is certainly not the Antichrist, but there is some logic to consider here. One thing the Antichrist absolutely will do is deceive. Scripture also tells us that in the last days many will fall away from the truth, not endure sound doctrine, and will accumulate for themselves teachers who will tell appeal to their *itching ears.*

Now it should make some sense. As false teachers go, Osteen may not be the worst of the lot, but he is - as we've seen - a false teacher. He does not preach the actual gospel, and he tells people only what they want to hear. Liking Joel Osteen is understandable, especially for folks who may not be well grounded in the scriptures, or perhaps have not even heard the real gospel. *(If they're listening to Osteen, they certainly haven't heard the part about sin and repentance.)* I would propose that the people God gets most upset with, are the ones who know the gospel, they've heard the truth, and yet they choose to listen to unbiblical ear candy like Osteen for the obvious reasons; he tells them exactly what they want to hear.

These people - *who have heard the truth* - should know better. The message of Osteen - as well as that of Joyce Meyer, Kenneth Copeland, Creflo Dollar, Bill Johnson and so many others - does not concur with Scripture and is definitely not the gospel as passed down by the Apostles. Yet it appeals to the carnal man and to the ego; people want to have their blessings in heaven, as well as right now, and scripture does not promise that. You will never hear a Joel Osteen preach on how we must carry our cross and die to self, as Jesus taught. In fact, that is the polar opposite of Osteen's standard thrust; his message is all about self! Therefore, God - knowing these people have heard the truth, yet would rather hear the opposite - sends them a strong delusion; Christian-*sounding* preachers who will tell them that they can have their cake and eat it too when God's Word paints a very different picture of what the Christian life should look like.

The idea that followers of false teachers have brought God's judgment upon themselves is a hard pill to swallow. Many of us feel understandably sorry for the folks who are being deceived. But once again, I believe scripture is talking about those who have heard the truth and would prefer to hear false comforts instead. It's as if God is saying, "I gave you the truth, but you want *that*? Okay, here it is...right now on TBN!"

EXCURSION APOCALYPTIC END TIMES: Exposing "the Man of Lawlessness"

THE ANTICHRIST & THE MAN OF LAWLESSNESS

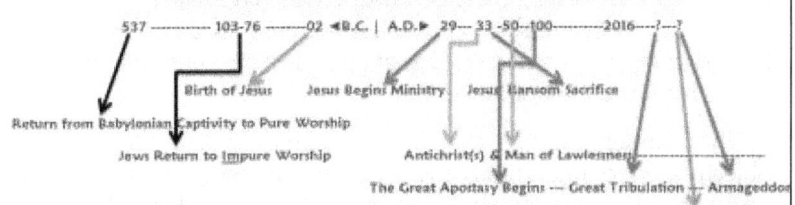

```
537 ---------- 103-76 -------- 02 ◄B.C. | A.D.► 29--- 33 -50--100---------2016----?---?
                    Birth of Jesus    Jesus Begins Ministry   Jesus Ransom Sacrifice
Return from Babylonian Captivity to Pure Worship
        Jews Return to Impure Worship            Antichrist(s) & Man of Lawlessness
                                        The Great Apostasy Begins --- Great Tribulation --- Armageddon
                                                                        The Second Coming of Christ
```

This **Man of Lawlessness** and the **Antichrist** is a religious rebellion, revolt against the Father the Son and the true Christians which would exist until the second coming of Jesus Christ. However, the true identity will be known at the end of the Last Days. The Last Days run from the day of Jesus' ransom sacrifice up unto the Second Coming of Christ.

2 Thessalonians 2:3-12 Updated American standard Version (UASV)

The Man of Lawlessness

³ Let no one deceive[79] you in any way, for it will not come unless the apostasy[80] comes first, and the man of lawlessness is revealed, the son of destruction, ⁴ who opposes and exalts himself against every so-called god or object of worship, so that he takes his seat in the temple of God, showing himself as being God. ⁵ Do you not remember that while I was still with you, I was telling you these things? ⁶ And now you know the thing restraining him, so that in his time he will be revealed. ⁷ For the mystery[81] of lawlessness is already at work; but only until the one who is right now acting as a restraint is out of the way. ⁸ **Then the lawless one will be revealed**, whom the Lord Jesus will do away with by the spirit of his mouth, and wipe out by the appearance[82] of his coming,[83] ⁹ namely, the one whose coming[84] is in accordance with the activity of Satan, with all power and signs and false wonders, ¹⁰ and with every unrighteous deception[85] for those who are perishing, because they did not receive the love of the truth so as to be saved. ¹¹ For this reason God is sending upon them a powerful delusion[86] so that they will believe the lie, ¹² in order that they all may be judged because they did not believe the truth but took pleasure in unrighteousness.

2 Thessalonians 2:8 Updated American Standard Version (UASV)

⁸ **Then the lawless one will be revealed**, whom the Lord Jesus will do away with by the spirit of his mouth, and wipe out by the appearance of his presence,

When we think of the past year, in the news media, we have witnessed atrocious cases of lawlessness around the world. We have seen hundreds of young ones killed in gang violence here in the United States. We have witnessed videos of the Islamic terrorist group known as ISIS, where hundreds of women and children have been raped and murdered, Christians have been beheaded and burned alive. However, there has been a far more treacherous lawless element that has been at work behind the scenes, truly going unnoticed for many centuries. In the Bible, it is called, "the man of lawlessness."

It is imperative that we identify this man of lawlessness. Why? His objective is to undermine the righteous standing of every genuine Christian and cost them their hope of everlasting life. How does the man of lawlessness accomplish such a task? He does so by getting Christians to abandon the truth for the lie. Jesus said, "true worshipers will worship the Father in spirit and truth." (John 4:23) It is the man of lawlessness' mission to get us away from our pure worship. He is in opposition to God and His purposes and is adamantly opposed to his dedicated worshippers. If any of us is so bold as to believe we are above being misled, we are just the ones he is looking for, as "pride goes before destruction, and a haughty spirit before a fall." – Proverbs 16:18, ESV.

---

[79] Or *seduce*

[80] **Apostasy**: (Gr. *apostasia*) The term literally means "to stand away from" and is used to refer to ones who 'stand away from the truth.' It is abandonment, a rebellion, an apostasy, a refusal to accept or acknowledge true worship. In Scripture, this is used primarily concerning the one who rises up in defiance of the only true God and his people, working in opposition to the truth.–Ac 21:21; 2 Thess. 2:3.

[81] **Mystery; Secret**: (Gr. *mystērion*) A sacred divine mystery or secret doctrine that lies with God alone, which is withheld from both the angelic body and humans, until the time he determines that it is to be revealed, and to those to whom he chooses to make it known.– Mark 4:11; Rom. 11:25; 16:25; 1 Cor. 2:1; 4:1; 13:2; 14:2; 15:51; Eph. 1:9; 6:19; Col. 1:26; 2:2; 2 Thess. 2:7; 1 Tim. 3:9; Rev. 17:5.

[82] **Appearing**: (Gr. *epiphaneia*) It literally means "a shining forth," which was used to refer to a divine being becoming visible to humans. *Epiphaneia* is used in the NT to refer to Jesus first coming to the earth and his second coming as well. – 2 Thess. 2:8; 1 Tim. 6:14; 2 Tim. 1:10; 4:1, 8.

[83] **Presence; Coming**: (Gr. *parousia*) The Greek word which is rendered as "presence" is derived from *para*, meaning "with," and *ousia*, meaning "being." It denotes both an "arrival" and a consequent "presence with." Depending on the context, it can mean "presence," "arrival," "appearance," or "coming." In some contexts, this word is describing the presence of Jesus Christ in the last days, i.e., from his ascension in 33 C.E. up unto his second coming, with the emphasis being on his second coming, the end of the age of Satan's reign of terror over the earth. We do not know the day nor the hours of this second coming. (Matt 24:36) It covers a marked period of time with the focus on the end of that period. – Matt. 24:3, 27, 37, 39; 1 Cor. 15:23; 16:17; 2 Cor. 7:6-7; 10:10; Php 1:26; 2:12; 1 Thess. 2:19; 3:13; 4:15; 5:2.

[84] See note on 2:8.

[85] Lit *seduction*

[86] Or *a deluding influence*; Lit *an operation of deceit*

2 Thessalonians 2:3 Updated American Standard Version (UASV)

³ Let no one deceive[87] you in any way, for it [the Lord's day of destruction of ungodly men] will not come unless the apostasy[88] comes first, and the man of lawlessness is revealed, the son of destruction,

Paul prophesied that an apostasy would develop and before that apostasy would be brought to an end the man of lawlessness would come. In fact, in verse 7 Paul stated, "For the mystery of lawlessness is already at work ..." Notice that, just like the antichrist, in the first century, this man of lawlessness was already making himself known.

Origin of the Lawless Man

2 Thessalonians 2:9-10 Updated American Standard Version (UASV)

⁹ namely, the one whose coming[89] is in accordance with the activity of Satan, with all power and signs and false wonders, ¹⁰ and with every unrighteous deception[90] for those who are perishing, because they did not receive the love of the truth so as to be saved.

We see here that is Satan, who originated this lawless man. Satan, the father of the lie, is also the one who has and who will continue to sustain the lawless one. In addition, just as Satan is an enemy of God and his people, so too, this man of lawlessness.

2 Thessalonians 2:8 Updated American Standard Version (UASV)

⁸ Then the lawless one will be revealed, whom the Lord Jesus will do away with by the spirit of his mouth, and wipe out by the appearance of his presence,

This man of lawlessness has but one future, i.e., destruction, along with anyone who goes along with him.

2 Thessalonians 1:6-9 Updated American Standard Version (UASV)

⁶ since indeed God considers it just to repay with affliction those who afflict you, ⁷ and to give relief to you who are afflicted along with us when the Lord Jesus will be revealed from heaven with His mighty angels in flaming fire, ⁸ in flaming fire, inflicting vengeance on those who do not know God and on those who do not obey the gospel of our Lord

---

[87] Or *seduce*

[88] **Apostasy:** (Gr. *apostasia*) The term literally means "to stand away from" and is used to refer to ones who 'stand away from the truth.' It is abandonment, a rebellion, an apostasy, a refusal to accept or acknowledge true worship. In Scripture, this is used primarily concerning the one who rises up in defiance of the only true God and his people, working in opposition to the truth. – Ac 21:21; 2 Thess. 2:3.

[89] See note on 2:8.

[90] Lit *seduction*

Jesus. ⁹ These ones will pay the penalty of eternal destruction, from before the Lord[91] and from the glory of his strength,

Paul gives further information in helping his readers to identify this man of lawlessness.

2 Thessalonians 2:4 Updated American Standard Version (UASV)

the son of destruction, ⁴ who opposes and exalts himself against every so-called god or object of worship, so that he takes his seat in the temple of God, showing himself as being God.

Here we see that Satan will raise up this lawless man, making him a false object of reverence, who will even place himself above God. On this Knute Larson writes, "This man will oppose everything connected with the divine–not only Christianity but anything that has to do with theism. This man will wage war against everything that hints at religion, faith, or spirituality. He will try to eradicate worship of any kind: prayers, songs, gatherings, and shrines."

He goes on saying, "The man of sin will set himself up **in God's temple**, or more literally, put himself into God's seat in the inner sanctuary of the temple, **proclaiming himself to be God**. This will be more than a taking over of some building. The man of sin will understand the implications and claims that attend taking his seat in the sanctuary of God. He will anoint himself as divine. He will usurp the rightful place of God and declare himself as the one to be worshiped." (Larson 2000, 106)

This lawless one is a hypocrite, a false teacher claiming to be Christian, who "takes his seat in the temple of God," namely, what such false teachers claim to be that temple.

Identifying the Lawless Man

Just like the antichrist, we have to ask, are we looking for a single individual? Was Paul speaking of just one person, who would be this man of lawlessness? No, for if he were just one person, he would have to be able to go without dying. Paul had stated that the man of lawlessness was "already at work" in Paul's day, and would be at work up unto the Lord's day of the destruction of ungodly men, that is, beyond the day of the penning of this book, which would make the lawless one almost 2,000 years old. Apparently, no ordinary man has lived that long. Therefore, the expression man of lawlessness must be composite, standing for a body or class of people.

---

[91] Lit *from before the face of the Lord*

Who are these ones that have been "at work" since Paul's day and are still "at work" in our day? Clearly, they are a body of arrogant, proud, self-important, self-righteous, ambitious leaders within false Christianity, who over the centuries have had great power within Satan's world, placing themselves above God and his Word. This author has written extensively about the fact that 41,000 different Christian denominations call themselves the truth and the way. Consider the fact that, they all have ministers, clergy, priests, elders, pastors, yet each conflicting with the others in some aspect of doctrine or practice. Many are actually in opposition to God's law, personality, standards, ways, and will, so, in effect, they are in opposition to God himself. (See Mark 3:24; Romans 16:17; 1 Corinthians 1:10) Many of these denominations do not keep hold of what the Bible really teaches. They have violated the principle of what Paul spoke of, 'not going beyond what is written.' (1 Cor. 4:6, ESV) In principle, the words of Jesus to the Jewish religious leaders of his day, wherein there were many different sects of Judaism, has much to offer us. He said, "And why do you break the commandment of God for the sake of your tradition?" (Matt 15:3, ESV) He went on to say, "in vain do they worship me, teaching as doctrines the commandments of men." (15:9) Lastly, Jesus said, "they are blind guides. And if the blind lead the blind, both will fall into a pit." – Matthew 15:14.

. So, again, this man of lawlessness is a composite person. The false religious leaders within Christianity, who are being used by Satan whether they are aware of it or not. Of these lawless ones, be it the Pope, Cardinals, Bishops, preachers, ministers, elders, or pastors, they will share in the destruction of the man of lawlessness, for their sins. Worse still, those within the churches, who make up the flocks of these false religious leaders of Christendom, will also share in the Lord's day of the destruction of ungodly men. King David wrote, "I do not sit with men of falsehood, nor do I consort with hypocrites." (Psa. 26:4, ESV) If one of God's holy ones are in one of these false denominations that call themselves Christian, God will offer them deliverance. The Palmist also wrote, "Hate evil, you who love the Lord, Who preserves the souls of His godly ones; He delivers them from the hand of the wicked." (Psa. 97:10, NASB) Jesus spoke of those who believed they were on the correct path, but, in fact, they were not. Jesus said,

Matthew 7:21-23 Updated American Standard Version (UASV)

[21] "Not everyone who says to me, 'Lord, Lord,' will enter the kingdom of heaven, but the one who does the will of my Father who is in heaven. [22] On that day many will say to me, 'Lord, Lord, did we not prophesy in your name, and cast out demons in your name, and do

many mighty works in your name?' ²³ And then I will declare to them, 'I never knew you; depart from me, you who practice lawlessness.'

Learning a Lesson from the Apostle Paul

The actual way to God was through the Israelite nation for over 1,500 years. When Jesus arrived he began what would become known as Christianity, his followers being called Christian.

Matthew 9:16-17 Updated American Standard Version (UASV)

¹⁶ But no one puts a patch of unshrunk cloth on an old garment; for the patch pulls away from the garment, and the tear becomes worse. ¹⁷ Nor do they put new wine into old wineskins. If they do, then the wineskins burst and the wine spills out and the wineskins are ruined. But they do put new wine into new wineskins, and both are preserved."

Jesus was making a point to the disciples of John the Baptist that no one should expect the followers of Jesus Christ to try to retain the old practices of Judaism, such as a ritualistic fasting. A Christian can fast if he chooses to do so, but there are no obligations to do so. Jesus did not come to patch up the old ways of worship by way of Judaism, which would be set aside on the day of Jesus' ransom sacrifice. Christianity is not to conform to the old way of worship, to the form Jewish religious system, with the traditions of men.

As Jesus said, Christianity was not going to be a new patch on an old garment or a new wine in an old wineskin. Any Christian or so-called Jewish Christian, who tries to suggest the mixing of the two is nothing more than false prophets. – Matthew 24:11.

We can define antichrist as anyone, any group, any organization, or any government that is *against* or *instead of* Christ, or who mistreat his people. Thus, we are not just looking for one person, one group, one organization, or one power. The Bible does not refer to just one antichrist. The greatest misidentification has been the interpretation that the Antichrist and the man of lawlessness is just one particular person.

Our Point Begins with Paul

Paul, who as we know was known as Saul before becoming the apostle Paul. Nevertheless, the objective way of believing certain Bible doctrines as being the truth is as follows. The biblical view of the doctrine _____ is _____, and it is the truth, unless, enough evidence comes along to say otherwise. If we grow in knowledge and understanding, our conclusions based on previous knowledge may need to be revised. For increased knowledge can require adjustments in one's thinking. We must remember the Apostle Paul studied under the renowned Pharisee Gamaliel, who was the grandson of Hillel, the Elder (110 B.C.E.[92] – 10 C.E.), the founder of one of the two schools within Judaism. Paul describes himself as "circumcised on the eighth day, of the people of Israel, of the tribe of Benjamin, a Hebrew of Hebrews; as to the law, a Pharisee; as to zeal, a persecutor of the church; as to righteousness under the law, blameless." (Phil 3:5-6) He also states, "But whatever gain I had, I counted as loss for the sake of Christ. Indeed, I count everything as loss because of the surpassing worth of knowing Christ Jesus my Lord. For his sake I have suffered the loss of all things and count them as rubbish, in order that I may gain Christ" (Phil. 3:7-8) Thus, we know that the Israelites were God's chosen people and the only way to God for some 1,500 years.

However, Jesus brought a new way, Christianity. Saul/Paul was slow to accept this because he could not see Jesus Christ as the long-awaited Messiah. Nevertheless, after Jesus visited Paul on the road to Damascus and Ananias, a Christian disciple of Damascus, visited Paul, he saw the Old Testament Scriptures pointing to the Messiah accurately, he was able to humble himself and accept a different belief, i.e., Christianity was the truth and the way.

To believe without enough support, to believe in the face of contrary evidence is irrational. Therefore, we must humbly examine the facts behind what we believe, to establish the truth continually. Just as the apostle Paul exhorted the Christians at Corinth to "examine yourselves, to see whether you are in the faith. Test yourselves." (2 Cor. 13:5) We could say the very same thing about our beliefs. We could say, 'examine our beliefs, to see whether they are the truth, test our beliefs.'

Now, this is not to suggest that our beliefs are to be ever changing, but that they should be able to stand up to scrutiny when they are challenged by something we have heard or read. However, this refinement of our beliefs should not be confused with allowing unfounded, damaging doubts to grow in our hearts and minds, doubts that can destroy our confidently established beliefs and our relationship with our heavenly Father. **Unfounded doubt** is defined as something that is not supported by any evidence or a minuscule amount of evidence, to cause uncertainty of belief or opinion that often interferes with our decision-making skills.

Our Point Ends with Us

We need to dig deeper into biblical truths, not as a sign of unfounded doubt but to make sure what we believe is so. If we think

---

[92] B.C.E. years ran down toward zero, although the Romans had no zero, and C.E. years ran up from zero. (100, 10, 3, 2, 1 ◀B.C.E. | C.E.▶ 1, 2, 3, 10, and 100)

that we can survive off the basic Bible knowledge that we acquired in the beginning and the simple snacks we receive at each Christian meeting, we are sadly mistaken because our spiritual health will deteriorate. It would be similar to our believing that we could maintain our physical health by only eating here and there.

Acts 17:10-11 Updated American Standard Version (UASV)

Paul and Silas in Berea

¹⁰ The brothers immediately sent Paul and Silas away by night to Berea, and when they arrived, they went into the synagogue of the Jews. ¹¹ Now these were more noble-minded than those in Thessalonica, for they received the word with great eagerness, examining the Scriptures daily to see whether these things were so.

Note that they **(1)** "received the word with all eagerness," and then went about **(2)** "examining the Scriptures daily to see if these things were so." If the apostle Paul was to be examined to see if what he said was so, surely uninspired commentators must be examined as well.

1 Timothy 1:13 Updated American Standard Version (UASV)

¹³ although formerly I [Saul/Paul] was a blasphemer, and a persecutor, and a violent man. But I was shown mercy because I had **acted unknowingly** with a lack of trust,

Suppose we **do not** realize that our particular Christian denomination or our Christian leader is a false teacher. Does our failing to reject it necessarily free us from further responsibility in the matter? If God continues to send us holy ones who attempt to share biblical truths be it by book, magazines, the internet, or even in person and we ignore such ones, we are sharing in the sins of others, which is a sin in and of itself. – 2 John 1:9-11.

Romans 10:2-3 Updated American Standard Version (UASV)

² For I [Saul/Paul] bear them witness that they [the Jews] have a zeal for God, but not according to accurate knowledge.[93] ³ For, being ignorant of the righteousness of God, and seeking to establish their own, they did not submit to God's righteousness.[94]

---

[93] *Epignosis* is a strengthened or intensified form of *gnosis* (*epi*, meaning "additional"), meaning, "true," "real," "full," "complete" or "accurate," depending upon the context. Paul and Peter alone use *epignosis*.

[94] **10:3 ignorant of God's righteousness**. Ignorant both of God's inherent righteousness revealed in the law and the rest of the OT (which should have shown the Jews their own unrighteousness) and of the righteousness which comes from Him on the basis of faith (see note on 1:17). **their own righteousness**. Based on their conformity to God's law and often to the less demanding standards of their own traditions (Mark 7:1–13). MacArthur, John (2005-

What has been demonstrated here thus far? Just because one is very active in their Christian denomination or church, this activity does not guarantee that they are receiving God's approval or that they are doctrinally correct. See Jesus words below for those who believed that they were in an approved relationship. It takes real heart and character to accept that one may be on the wrong path when it comes to long-held biblical beliefs. It takes an act of humility to accept that we may need to make an adjustment in our view of a certain doctrine. Jesus words from above bear repeating.

Matthew 7:21-23 Updated American Standard Version (UASV)

[21] "Not everyone who says to me, 'Lord, Lord,' will enter the kingdom of heaven, but the one who does the will of my Father who is in heaven. [22] On that day many will say to me, 'Lord, Lord, did we not prophesy in your name, and cast out demons in your name, and do many mighty works in your name?' [23] And then I will declare to them, 'I never knew you; depart from me, you who practice lawlessness.'

It was Saul/Paul's zeal and his conscience that was pricked to defend what he thought was the truth, and yet he openly admitted that he was over-zealous, that his zeal was misdirected, because of ignorance. This should cause us to pause and reflect. The presence of false teachers in the Christian congregation from the first century onward means that one cannot just naively accept that they are getting the truth. It would be foolish to assume such.

1 Thessalonians 5:21 Updated American Standard Version (UASV)

[21] But examine everything carefully; hold fast to that which is good;

The Greek word *dokimazete* rendered simply as "test" in the English Standard Version or the Holman Christian Standard Bible denotes a careful examination of "everything." If one is to make a careful examination of everything, it will require that they are not just passively going along, but rather, one should be buying out the time, to have an accurate understanding of God's Word, by doing an in-depth study of what they believe to be true.

Certainly, if what Paul had to say about the Scriptures was under examination, no one else is above having their beliefs examined. The Jews of Berea did not just accept what Paul was saying about the death and resurrection of Jesus, as being so. Moreover, Paul commended them for their due diligence. (See 17:3) This was no brief or superficial examination of the Scriptures either; they met **daily** to **examine** the

---

05-09). *The MacArthur Bible Commentary* (Kindle Locations 52230-52233). Thomas Nelson. Kindle Edition.

Scriptures. For the above reasons, it is only through living by faith and accurate knowledge that we can receive God's favor.

Pride and Haughtiness Is an Identifying Marker

The man of lawlessness throughout history has evidenced such pride, arrogance, and haughtiness that they have controlled world leaders. They have used the pretext of God's Word and Bible doctrines, they have controlled the masses, as well as an intermediary between the world leaders and God. For centuries, these false Christs have crowned and dethroned kings and emperors. In many ways, their words and deeds have been similar to those of the Jewish religious leaders of Jesus' day, "We have no king but Caesar." (John 19:15, ESV) However, Jesus words were far different, "My kingdom is not of this world." – John 18:36.

To place themselves above God's people, these false religious leaders, these men of lawlessness have adopted different clothing, which is usually black, and in some cases a white color around the neck. Keep in mind, others dress in $5,000 suits while their flocks are fleeced. Jesus and his disciples did no such thing. In fact, when Jesus was being arrested, Judas had to kiss him because he could not be distinguished from the others with him. Moreover, they have bestowed upon themselves titles such as "Father," "Holy Father," "Reverend," "Most Reverend," "His Excellency," and "His Eminence," when Jesus said, "call no man your father on earth, for you have one Father, who is in heaven." (Matt. 23:9) Remember, these ones are wolves in sheep's clothing.

In Matthew Chapter 7, Jesus started out by talking about two paths and false teachers. False teachers imply false teachings. Again, what did Jesus say he would say to those who thought they were doing the right thing or thought they were teaching the right thing but were not? 'I never knew you; depart from me, you workers of lawlessness.' (Matt. 7:23)

We have false teachers, who are difficult to recognize, as they appear as innocent as sheep. Recognizing them can only be accomplished by recognizing their fruit (words and deeds), as well as knowing the true will of the Father. Does it not then seem prudent on our behalf that we should apply,

2 Thessalonians 2:10 Updated American Standard Version (UASV)

[10] and with all wicked deception for those who are perishing, because they did not receive the love of the truth so as to be saved.

2 Corinthians 13:5 Updated American Standard Version (UASV)

⁵ Examine yourselves, to see whether you are in the faith. Test yourselves. Or do you not realize this about yourselves, that Jesus Christ is in you?–unless indeed you fail to meet the test!

Yes, the ones, who are deceived by these false teachers, will perish because refused to be receptive to the truth. Therefore, we need to be in a constant mode of examining ourselves, as well as our beliefs, to see whether we are really in the truth. We would be wise if we heed the insight from Paul to the Corinthians,

2 Corinthians 11:13-15 Updated American Standard Version (UASV)

¹³ For such men are false apostles, deceitful workers, disguising themselves as apostles of Christ. ¹⁴ And no wonder, for even Satan disguises himself as an angel of light. ¹⁵ Therefore it is not a great thing if his servants also disguise themselves as servants of righteousness, whose end will be according to their deeds.

Rejection of the Truth Is an Identifying Marker

The apostle Paul said that this man of lawlessness was going to grow with apostasy (rejection of the truth). Actually, the first sign Paul gave as to the identity of this lawless class is that "the day of the Lord [i.e., the day of judgment and destruction of ungodly men] ... will not come unless the apostasy comes first." (2 Thess. 2:2-3) What exactly did Paul mean by "apostasy"? He meant to stand off from the truth, i.e., to not only fall away from the faith but to then turn on the faith, rebellion. On this apostasy, Knute Larson writes,

Before that great day comes, Paul declared, the **rebellion** must occur. The word used here is *apostasia*, or apostasy. Before the day of the Lord, there will be a great denial, a deliberate turning away by those who profess to belong to Christ. It will be a rebellion. Having once allied themselves with Christ, they will abandon him. Within the recognized church there will come a time when people will forsake their faith. Throughout history there have been defections from the faith. But the apostasy about which he wrote to the Thessalonians would be of greater magnitude and would signal the coming of the end. (Larson 2000, 106)

The Great Apostasy

2 Thessalonians 2:1a, 3 Updated American Standard Version (UASV)

¹ Now we request you, brothers, with regard to the presence of our Lord Jesus Christ ... ³ Let no one deceive[95] you in any way, for it will not

---

[95] Or *seduce*

come **unless the apostasy comes first**, and the man of lawlessness is revealed, the son of destruction,

On this text, New Testament scholar Jon A. Weatherly writes, "Following the warning about deception, the rest of the verse in the Greek text is an anacoluthon, a subordinate clause with no clause to complete it. Literally, the text reads, 'Because unless the rebellion comes first and the man of lawlessness is revealed.' Translators must supply the clause introduced with 'because' (ὅτι, *hoti*), which can be clearly inferred from v. 2. Since the question concerns the coming of the day of the Lord, Paul apparently expects the reader to conclude that the day is preceded by the rebellion and revelation of the man of lawlessness."[96] (Weatherly 1996)

The apostle Paul says to the Ephesian elders; there is but "one Lord, one faith, one baptism." (Eph. 4:5) Paul penned those words about 60 C.E., and he was informing them that there was but one Christian faith. Yet, today we see more varieties of Christian faith than we care to count, all claiming that they are the truth and the way. Whenever a brave soul dares to be truthful and bring up that there are doctrinal differences, different doctrinal position, and different standards of conduct, he is shouted down as an alarmist. They claim that most of these denominations are the same on the essential doctrines, i.e., the salvation doctrines. Well, this actually is not true and is an attempt at hiding the truth, because even the salvation doctrines have anywhere from three to five different interpretations. Regardless, we must concern ourselves with a crucial question from Jesus Christ, "when the Son of Man comes, will he find faith on earth?" (Lu 18:8) This is a whole other discussion. We concern ourselves with how these divisions came about in the first place.

As has already been stated, but bears repeating, the blame lies with Satan. He attempted to have Jesus killed as a baby; he tempted Jesus in the wilderness after his baptism, and he attempted persecution right from the start. Peter wrote, "Be sober-minded; be watchful. Your adversary the devil prowls around like a roaring lion, seeking someone to devour." (1 Pet. 5:8) Initially, the persecution of this young Christian body came from Jewish religious leaders, and then from the Roman Empire itself. With "all authority in heaven" (Matt. 28:20) Jesus watched on, as the Holy Spirit guided and directed them, this infancy Christian congregation endured the best that Satan and his henchman had to offer. (See Rev. 1:9; 2:3, 19) As we know from Scripture, Satan is not one to give up, so he devised a new plan, divide and conquer. Yes, he would cause divisions within the Christian congregation. Satan broke out the ultimate

---

[96] Jon A. Weatherly, *1 & 2 Thessalonians*, The College Press NIV Commentary (Joplin, MO: College Press Pub. Co., 1996), 2 Th 2:3.

weapon – **the apostasy.**[97] We need not believe that all of a sudden the apostasy came into the Christian congregation. No, Jesus was watching from heaven, and he made sure that he warned them while he was here on earth of what was to come and he made the young Christian congregation aware of what was coming and when it was getting started. – Colossians 1:18.

"[Jesus] Be Aware of False Prophets …

[Peter] There Will Be False Teachers Among You"

Matthew 7:15 Updated American Standard Version (UASV)

[15] "Beware of the false prophets, who come to you in sheep's clothing, but inwardly are ravenous wolves."

Jesus was well aware of what Satan would try to accomplish step-by-step, and that divisions through those from within were on the list. New Testament scholar Stuart K. Weber says, "Jesus had an important reason for inserting the wolf metaphor (Acts 20:27-31)–to alert his listeners to the danger of a false prophet. If the false prophets were thought of as a source of bad fruit, then the disciples might think it was enough simply to recognize and ignore the false prophet, refusing to consume his bad fruit, and awaiting God's judgment on him. But the wolf metaphor attributes a more active and malicious motive to the false prophet. He is actually an enemy of the sheep, and, if not confronted, will get his way by destroying the sheep." (Weber 2000, 101)

Weber mentions Acts 20:28-30, where Paul, about **56 C.E.,** warned the Ephesian elders,

Acts 20:28-30 Updated American Standard Version (UASV)

[28] Pay careful attention to yourselves and to all the flock, in which the Holy Spirit has made you overseers, to care for the congregation of God, which he obtained with the blood of his own Son. [29] I know that after my departure fierce wolves will come in among you, not sparing the flock; [30] and **from among your own selves** men will arise, **speaking twisted things, to draw away the disciples after them.**

Yes, these, who stand off from the truth and the way, would not be seeking their own disciples, but rather they would be seeking, "to draw away the disciples [Jesus' disciples] after them." Jesus was well aware that the easiest way to defeat any group is to divide them, and so was Satan, who had been watching humanity for over 4,000 years, and

---

[97] In the Greek New Testament, the noun "apostasy" (Gr., *apostasia*) has the sense of "desertion, abandonment or rebellion." (Acts 21:21, ftn.) There it predominantly is alluding to abandonment; a drawing away from or abandoning of pure worship.

especially the Israelites (Isaac and Ishmael / Jacob and Esau / Israel and Judah), as "Satan disguises himself as an angel of light. So it is no surprise if his servants, also, disguise themselves as servants of righteousness." – 2 Corinthians 11:14-15.

There were even some divisions beginning as early as **49 C.E.**, when the elders wrote a letter to the Gentile believers, saying,

Acts 15:24 Updated American Standard Version (UASV)

24 Since we have heard that some went out from among us and troubled you with words, unsettling your souls,[98] although we gave them no instructions,

Here we see that some *within* [those who were Christians but had left the faith], were being very vocal about their opposition to the direction the faith was heading. Here, it was over whether the Gentiles needed to be circumcised, suggesting that they needed to be obedient to the Mosaic Law. – Acts 15:1, 5.

"[Paul says it] Is Already at Work."

About **51 C.E.**, some 18-years after Jesus' death, resurrection and ascension, division was already starting to creep into the faith, "the mystery of lawlessness **is already at work**." (2 Thess. 2:7) Yes, the power of **the man of lawlessness** was already present, which is the power of Satan, the god of this world (2 Cor. 4:3-4), and his tens of millions of demons, are hard at work behind the scenes.

The apostle Peter also spoke of these things about **64 C.E.**, "there will be false teachers among you, who will secretly bring in destructive heresies ... in their greed they will exploit you with false words.." (2 Pet. 2:1, 3) These abandoned the faithful words, became false teachers, rising within the Christian congregation, sharing their corrupting influence, intending to hide, disguise, or mislead.

These dire warnings by Jesus and the New Testament Authors had their beginnings in the first century C.E. Yes, they began small, but burst forth on the scene in the second century.

As the years progressed throughout the first-century, this divisive "talk [would] spread like gangrene." (2 Tim. 2:17, c. **65 C.E.**) About **51 C.E.**, They had some in Thessalonica, at worst, going ahead of, or at best, misunderstanding Paul, and wrongly stating by word and a bogus letter "that the day of the Lord has come." (2 Thess. 2:1-2) In Corinth, about **55 C.E.**, "some of [were saying] that there is no resurrection of the

---

[98] This means that some, who left the Christian faith and were not trying to subvert (undermine) the faith of others.

dead. (1 Cor. 15:12) About **65 C.E.**, some were "saying that the resurrection has already happened. They [were] upsetting the faith of some." – 2 Timothy 2:16-18.

Throughout the next three decades, **no** inspired books were written. However, by the time of the apostle John's letter writing days of 96-98 C.E., he tells us "Now many antichrists have come. Therefore we know that it is the last hour." (1 John 2:18) These are ones, "who denies that Jesus is the Christ" and ones who not confess "Jesus Christ has come in the flesh is from God." – 1 John 2:22; 4:2-3.

From 33 C.E. to 100 C.E., the apostles served Christ as a restraint against "the apostasy" that was coming. Paul stated at 2 Thessalonians 2:7, "For the mystery of lawlessness is already at work; but only until the one who is right now acting as a restraint [Jesus' apostles] is out of the way." 2 Thessalonians 2:3 said, "Let no one deceive you in any way [misinterpretation or false teachers of Paul's first letter], for it will not come unless the apostasy comes first, and the man of lawlessness [composite person, or maybe an organization/movement, empowered by Satan] is revealed, the son of destruction."

So, again, how did this apostasy, this rebellion, grow out of the first-century Christian congregation? Repeating Paul's words to Thessalonica about "the thing that acts as a restraint" on the lawless one. We have already said that it was the apostles, who acted as this restraining force. It was the presence of the apostles, with the powerful gift of the Holy Spirit, which held off the apostasy in its full force. (Acts 2:1-4; 1 Cor. 12:28) Nevertheless, when the last apostle John died in about 100 C.E., this restraint was removed. Again, we look at an example, from the words of New Testament textual scholar, Philip W. Comfort,

Once the final, authorized publication was released and distributed to the churches, I think it unlikely that any substantive changes would have occurred during the lifetime of the apostles or second-generation coworkers. By "substantive," I mean a change that would alter Christian doctrine or falsify an apostolic account. The primary reason is that the writers (or their immediate successors) were alive at the time and therefore could challenge any significant, unauthorized alterations. As long as eyewitnesses such as John or Peter were alive, who would dare change any of the Gospel accounts in any significant manner? Anyone among the Twelve could have testified against any falsification. And there was also a group of 72 other disciples (Luke 10:1) who could do the same. Furthermore, according to 1 Corinthians 15:6, Jesus had at least five hundred followers by the time he had finished his ministry, and these people witnessed Jesus in resurrection. Most of these people were still alive (Paul said) in **AD 57/58** (the date of composition for 1 Corinthians);

it stands to reason that several lived for the next few decades—until the turn of the century and even beyond.[99]

We must keep in mind that the meaning of any given text is what the author meant by the words that he used, as should have been understood by his audience, and had some relevance/meaning for his audience. The rebellion [apostasy] began slowly in the first century and would break forth after the death of the last apostle, i.e., John. As the historian, Ariel Durant informed us earlier, by 187 C.E., there were 20 varieties of Christianity, and by 384 C.E., there were 80 varieties of Christianity. Christianity would become one again, a universal religion, i.e., Catholicism.

Gnostic Belief

Marcion (85-c.160) was a semi-Gnostic, who believed that the teachings of Jesus were irreconcilable with the actions of the God of the Old Testament. He viewed the God of the Old Testament, Jehovah, to be vicious, violent and cruel, an oppressor who gave out material rewards to those worshiping him. In contrast, Marcion described the New Testament God, Jesus Christ, as a perfect God, the God of unadulterated love and compassion, of kindness and quick to forgive.

Montanus (late second century) was a "prophet" from Asia Minor, who believed that their revelation came directly from the Holy Spirit, which superseded the authority of Jesus, Paul, Peter, John, James, anyone really. They believed in the imminent return of Christ and the setting up of the New Jerusalem in Pepuza. He was more concerned about Christian conduct than he was Christian doctrine, wanting to get back to the Christian values of the first century. However, he took this to the extreme, just as John Calvin would some 1,300 years later in the 16th century. Montanism was a movement focused on prophecy, especially the founder's views, being seen as the light for their time. They believed that the apostle and prophets had the power to forgive sin.

Valentinus (c.100-c.160) was a Greek poet, who founded his school in Rome and most prominent early Christian gnostic theologian. He claimed that though Jesus' heavenly (spiritual) body was of Mary, he was not actually born from her. This belief came about because Gnostics viewed all matter as evil. Therefore, if Jesus had really been a real human person with a physical body, he would have been evil. Another form of Gnosticism was Docetism, which claimed that Jesus Christ was not a real

---

[99] Philip Comfort, *Encountering the Manuscripts: An Introduction to New Testament Paleography & Textual Criticism* (Nashville, TN: Broadman & Holman, 2005), 255–256.

person, i.e., it was mere appearance and illusion, which would have included his death and resurrection.

Manes (c. 216-274) was the prophet and the founder of Manichaeism, a gnostic religion. He sought to combine elements of Christianity, Buddhism, and Zoroastrianism, based on a rigid dualism of good and evil, locked in an eternal struggle. He believed that salvation is possible through education, self-denial, fasting, and chastity. He also believed that he was an "apostle of Jesus Christ," (Ramsey 2006, 272) although, strictly speaking, his religion was not a movement of Christian Gnosticism in the earlier approach.

Beginning with the Council of Nicaea in 325 C.E., Emperor Constantine legalized Christianity in an attempt at reunited the empire. He thoroughly understood that religious division was a threat to the continuation of the Roman Empire. However, it was Emperor Theodosius I (347 – 395 C.E.), who banned paganism and imposed Christianity as the State religion of the Roman Empire. The Roman Catholic Church can trace its existence back to the council of Nicaea in 325 C.E. at best. Protestantism had its beginnings in the Reformation of the 16th century. However, there were dissensions in within Catholicism for a thousand years. Another identifying marker was the unscriptural clergy class that would develop over the coming centuries after the Council of Nicaea. This relegated the Christians to a second-class status. This is the way, the apostate; the man of lawlessness slowly took the reins of power. It was Constantine the Great, who legalized Christianity, but it was Theodosius I (d. 395 C.E.), who made Christianity a state religion. For centuries there was the Holy Roman Empire (5th to the 15th century C.E.),[100] which was anything but holy. As schisms and rifts took place, Christianity fragmented into tens of thousands of denominations. An example of such glorification by the man of lawlessness, setting oneself up over God is that of the papacy of Rome.

Lucio Ferraris in his *Ecclesiastical Dictionary*, which was used as a standard for Roman Catholic divinity, offers its readers the following on papal power, "The pope is of such dignity and highness, that he is not simply man, but, as it were, God, and the vicar of God. Ferraris goes on, "The pope is father of fathers; since he possesses the primacy over all, is truly greater than all, and the greatest of all. He is called most holy because he is presumed to be such ... Hence the pope is crowned with the triple crown as king of heaven, of earth and of hell ... he is also above angels and is their superior ... He is of such great dignity and power that he occupies one and the same tribunal with Christ; so that whatever the pope does, seems to proceed from the

---

[100] The precise term "Holy Roman Empire" was not used until the 13th century.

mouth of God." Ferraris in his Ecclesiastical Dictionary goes on saying, "God on earth, the only prince of the faithful of Christ, the greatest king of all kings, possessing the plentitude of power, to whom the government of the earthly and heavenly kingdom is [entrusted]. (Elliott 1941, 157)

Let us consider the humble words of Peter, who said to the Roman army officer Cornelius, who "fell down at his feet and worshiped him," "Stand up, . . . I am only a man after all"! (Acts 10:25-26, the Catholic Jerusalem Bible) Then there is the humility of an angel when the apostle John bowed down in a worshipful attitude before him. The angel said, "You must not do that! I am a fellow servant with you and your brothers the prophets, and with those who keep the words of this book. Worship God." – Revelation 22:8-9, ESV.

While we have covered Catholicism and the pope, the question that many might have is, 'have the Protestant denominations faired any better?' The answer is actually a mixed review in that "yes" in a small way and "no" in a major way. One of the major contributions of the Protestant Reformation was that these men gave us the Bible in our common languages, be it French, German, English, etc. Another benefit was the abandonment of many of the false doctrines of the Catholic Church, such as transubstantiation, Mary as the mother of God, apostolic succession, among so many others. The third greatest contribution was the search for biblical truths. However, we must note that many of the excellent reasons for rebelling against the Catholic Church were short-lived, as the fragmentation of denominations grew even faster after the Reformation. Most Protestant denominations have no reliable way of interpreting the Scriptures. Most use historical-critical methods of interpretation, which is subject and allows the reader to determine the meaning while few denominations use the historical-grammatical method, which is objective, and the meaning is drawn from what the author meant. Several books have been written on this issue alone.

Much of Protestantism has failed to affirm Scripture as inspired, fully inerrant and authoritative. In addition, many denominations have abandoned the Word of God by leaving the literal translation philosophy for an interpretive translation known as the dynamic or functional equivalent.[101] These ones would argue that the Bible is full of errors, contradiction, myths, and legends. Many would argue that Moses is not the author of the first five book but rather several authors penned the book from the 10th and 5th centuries B.C.E. Many would argue that

---

[101] Do We Still Need a Literal Bible?: Discover the Truth about Literal Bibles Authored by Don Wilkins http://www.christianpublishers.org/apps/webstore/products/show/4676433

there are three authors, who penned the book, which we know as Isaiah, and none is the Isiah of the 8th-century B.C.E. They claim that Daniel did not write the book bearing his name, as it was written centuries later. Many more similar points could be made. As has been stated, the Protestant denominations cannot preserve any unity in their doctrinal views. Protestantism has failed to have any cohesion or to carry out the one commission that Jesus Christ gave: to proclaim the Gospel, teach Bible doctrines and to make disciples. They have failed to evangelize in their own communities. They have failed to teach the Bible to their own flock, as over ninety percent of churchgoers are biblically illiterate.

New Testament textual scholar Daniel B. Wallace writes, "In Protestantism, one really doesn't know what he or she will experience from church to church. Even churches of the same denomination are widely divergent. Some have a rock-solid proclamation of the Word, while others play games and woo sinners to join their ranks without even the slightest suggestion that they should repent of anything. Too many Protestant churches look like social clubs where the offense of the gospel has been diluted to feel-good psycho-theology. And the problem is only getting worse with mega-churches with their mini-theology. This ought not to be."[102]

Is this evaluation or appraisal of Catholicism and Protestantism too strong? Before we answer that, let it be said, Catholicism is a part of the composite body of the man of lawlessness, so there is no help that Titanic of a religious organization from going down but we can help those within, to find their way to the correct path, which leads to life. Besides, the vast majority of Protestantism is also a part of that body or composite of the man of lawlessness. Again, we cannot save the huge organization from going under, but we can pull members off their ship before it goes down in destruction with the ungodly men. However, I do believe God is using Protestantism in the sense that the true church will be identifiable before the end comes and those loving the truth will be able to make the choice to follow God or follow traditions.

If we are to identify whether our church or our denomination is a part of the man of lawlessness, we must apply the rule that Jesus gave for identifying false prophets. He said,

Matthew 7:15-16 Updated American Standard Version (UASV)

15 "Beware of the false prophets, who come to you in sheep's clothing, but inwardly are ravenous wolves. 16 You will recognize them

---

[102] The Problem With Protestant Ecclesiology — Fr. John Peck, http://frjohnpeck.com/the-problem-with-protestant-ecclesiology/ (accessed January 03, 2016).

> by their fruits. They do not gather grapes from thorn bushes, or figs from thistles, do they? [17] So every good tree bears good fruit, but the bad tree bears bad fruit.
>
> We have spoken of the fruitage in the above. In the next Blog article, we will look more at these fruitages. We will talk more about the fate of the man of lawlessness and for those sharing in his sins. Moreover, we will consider what the responsibilities of true Christians are as to this lawless one.

Some Final Thoughts

We've seen a lot in this study, but we've just skimmed the surface of what is polluting the church today. In a nutshell, we're seeing a clearly false gospel, and a false Jesus being promoted in the presence of lying signs and wonders. We see a man-centered gospel devoid of preaching on sin and repentance. Rather than preaching the cross, we are just being told that God is love, and He wants you to enjoy your best life now. We see great deception in the form of miracles that are not from God. We see self-appointed apostles and prophets revealing things contrary to scripture and preaching a *Gospel of the Kingdom* that is diametrically opposed to biblical prophecies regarding the last days. We see false teachers proposing that Christians unite with apostate religious systems for the sake of unity. All this sounds alarmingly like what the Bible predicts will happen. Does it make sense to say that all this is just a matter of people being confused on doctrine and theology? Or does it make sense to say that all these things are leading people *away* from the Jesus of scripture, and *must*, therefore, be the deceptions of Satan? I am convinced that what we've examined is truly the end times work of Satan. When all is said and done - knowing what the Word of Faith and New Apostolic Reformation movements are all about, can you still be comfortable endorsing anyone who promotes such teachings? I know I can't.

What about Other Groups?

Some folks could reasonably ask why I am concentrating so much on false teachings within the charismatic movement? Surely other groups are out there promoting false gospels and false Christs? Absolutely true, but there's a very good reason why my focus has been where it has and will remain. False teachers within the Word of Faith, New Apostolic and extreme charismatic movements pose the greatest danger to the body of Christ because they convincingly disguise themselves as members of that body. Therefore, they pose the greatest risk of deception. Most born-again Christians already know that Catholics, Mormons, Jehovah's Witnesses, and those folks who may be cloistered in hiding, waiting for the flying saucers to come to take them away are not proclaiming the truth.

However, those who look, act and speak like Christians, yet are not, pose a very real threat to believers, and to those unsaved folks who may be interested in the gospel. There are massive numbers of people who are truly born again yet are being influenced by false teachers and have no clue that they are embracing heresy. As I stated earlier, they won't lose their salvation, but they will be filled with false hope based on empty promises, which can deliver a crushing blow to one's faith. And those folks who are unsaved may embrace a false Jesus and go through life thinking they're saved when they're not, which is a tragedy of eternal consequence.

Most believers are at a minimal risk of embracing falsehoods when the Mormons or the JW's[103] knock at their doors, yet they'll turn on TBN, hear a smooth Word of Faith preacher talking about Jesus, albeit a false Jesus, and be swayed to embrace a boatload of lies. Thus, I feel it is imperative that we shine the spotlight where we have; where the greatest danger lies. It's been said that Satan is not opposed to religion. Rather, he is creating a counterfeit Christianity that looks and sounds so much like the real thing, that even true believers will have great difficulty seeing the difference. That is why it is so important to sound the alarm regarding those who speak falsely of Christ while appearing to belong to Him. They must be exposed!

Ten Tips for Discernment

Discernment: (Heb. *tevunah*) This involves seeing or recognizing things, but it emphasizes distinguishing the parts, weighing or evaluating one in the light of the others. Pro. 2:3; 17:27; 21:30.

It cannot be stressed enough how important discernment is for today's believer. We have seen how smoothly and subtly false teachings and all manner of deceptions are creeping into the church today. With that in mind, I'd like to offer some closing thoughts on discernment.

1: KNOW YOUR BIBLE!

Satan knows scripture all too well. Just look at how he used it in the temptation of Jesus. He is a master of quoting Scriptures out of context and making them seem to say things they do not. There is no doubt he leads false teachers to do the same. We are very vulnerable to his tactics if we do not have a thorough knowledge of scripture and the doctrines it does and does not support. Too many Christians spend more time reading their

---

[103] CHRISTIAN APOLOGETIC EVANGELISM: What Will You Say to a Jehovah's Witness? https://christianpublishinghouse.co/2018/02/24/christian-apologetic-evangelism-what-will-you-say-to-a-jehovahs-witness/

favorite Christian authors than they do the Word of God. Find a way to make serious Bible study a priority.

2: TEST THE SPIRITS

Testing the spirits is vital and requires effort. I know people who claim to have tested the spirits because they looked at someone's statement of faith and it seemed legit; it even included some scriptures! Virtually *anyone* can produce a statement of faith that *appears* orthodox. You need to dig deeper, and it requires some work on your part. Google someone's name plus *teachings* and read some of the articles that come up. Not everything you see this way may be true, but if such a search leads to numerous articles warning about false teachings, that should be a red flag, and a clue to dig deeper. A point to remember is that a counterfeit is designed to look as much like the real thing as possible, and Satan does this quite well. People in the banking business learn how to spot fake money by being thoroughly familiar with the real thing. Christians need to do this as well by knowing their Bibles.

3: WHERE IS THE EMPHASIS?

Check out a person's website to get a feel for where their emphasis is. If possible, listen to some of their sermons. Are they stressing the gospel message of salvation through Christ... or something else? If you see an emphasis on anything other than the gospel, be it healing, prophecies, prosperity or so forth, your discernment meter should start to register something!

4: WHO'S GETTING THE GLORY?

At one of the Billy Burke services I attended, I saw something that I had never seen in a church service before and hope to never see again! The meeting, which was a Sunday morning service with his Tampa congregation, started normally enough with some worship songs followed by an offering. Then, someone took the stage and said, *"And now, will you please join me in welcoming our pastor...Billy Burke!"* The congregation stood up and gave him a *standing ovation!* This absolutely grieved and disgusted the spirit within me. Like I said - who's getting the glory?

5: CHECK OUT THEIR WEBPAGE

If someone's web page looks like a shrine to themselves, beware! I have discovered a habit among false teachers of plastering their own pictures, often in dramatic, spiritual-looking poses all over their web pages.

6: ODD PHRASES AND DISCLAIMERS

Watch out for phrases, instructions, and claims that don't sound biblical. One pastor I researched had a link on his page entitled, *Five Hindrances to Answered Prayer.* His first point was that God can't answer your prayer unless you speak it out loud. *(Would this mean that a mute person has no hope of crying out to God?)* That's a big red flag for Word of Faith heresies right there. God is omniscient. He knows our every thought without us needing to speak it. Another example was this same person stating that the Bible is the Word of God, but only if it's the King James version. We've already addressed how ridiculous that notion is. The King James version is perfectly fine but so are many other versions. There are a few paraphrases out there like *The Message* and *The Passion Translation*, which were created with an agenda to make the Bible appear to support doctrine which it does not. *The Passion Translation* even dares to add entire sentences and phrases that don't belong, in an effort to support the false teachings of the New Apostolic Reformation.

7: EMPHASIS ON GIVING

Giving to your church and to other legit ministries is a wonderful thing to do, but if you look at someone's web page and every half inch of space is populated by large font buttons labeled *GIVE*, use extreme caution.

8: SECRET KNOWLEDGE...FOR A PRICE!

False teachers tend to offer a plethora of merchandise, which often promises to reveal biblical secrets you can learn nowhere else, or the unraveling of supernatural mysteries via divine revelation to the author.

9: ASSOCIATIONS

If you're wondering about a certain teacher or pastor, look at who they associate with. If you see that they participate in conferences or other events with known false teachers, be wary! Most solid Bible teachers will not give an even tacit endorsement to a known false teacher.

10: MISUSE OR ABUSE OF SACRAMENTS

False teachers in the Word of Faith / NAR camp have an unfortunate tendency to misuse the sacraments in ways other than what scripture commands. For example, water baptism is simply a sign of obedience that we've died to sin and been raised to new life in Christ. I've seen an ocean baptism used as an excuse to allegedly impart healings, and give people a *powerful supernatural experience*, complete with people being slain in the spirit out in the ocean! I overheard people saying they come to get baptized every year, to *experience the power*. This is not at all biblical, and while scripture doesn't specifically address the issue, I'd guess the

Lord isn't too pleased with people using baptism for sensationalism! I've also seen people who desired healing be encouraged to take communion every day at home because communion *opens a door to the supernatural*. No, it doesn't; if it does, then scripture forgot to mention it. The Last Supper observance is to commemorate what the Lord did for us.

There's nothing wrong with taking communion at home for the right reasons, but to think it's a mystical rite for receiving miracles is just plain wrong. Of course, the charlatan encouraging this also sells pricey communion sets on his website. What a surprise.

CONCLUSION After Thoughts

Perhaps you've seen yourself somewhere in the previous pages. The Word of Faith, extremely charismatic, and New Apostolic Reformation movements have left a multitude of confused and discouraged believers in their wake. Some folks have been so damaged and shattered from the empty hopes and false promises they once embraced, that they have abandoned God altogether, or struggled to maintain their faith despite feeling deep depression and discouragement. Maybe you're just starting to sense that some of the things you've been led to believe are not true. Learning that teachers and pastors you once trusted have been lying to you is bound to cause a great deal of cognitive dissonance, as is learning that many scripture passages do not mean what you've been told they mean.

But you are not alone. There are many, many scarred and damaged people coming out of these spiritually manipulative, abusive, and deceitful belief systems. Shattered faith and discouragement is the norm for such folks. Some people need to avail themselves of wise counsel from biblically sound pastors to help heal their damaged souls and emotions. There is no shame in that. Many false teachers have an almost cult-like hold over their followers and the need for some type of "deprogramming" is real!

But what is also real is that the good news of the gospel is true! The true God of scripture is infinitely more powerful than the limited "God" of the false movements we've discussed. He is absolutely in control and loves us so much that He took on human form in the person of Jesus - fully God and fully man - and atoned for our sins on the cross. He arose from the grave on the third day, victorious over sin and death. Our salvation is His gift to us. We can do nothing to earn it. If we place our faith in Him and what He did for us by His grace and turn from our sins, we are born again and assured of eternity in His presence.

No, this life is not promised to be all rainbows and puppies; there will be hardships in life. There will be sickness and trials. There is no guarantee that we will always be spared from these things. But we must remember to look at life from the perspective of eternity. This life may seem hard, yet it is but a vapor that vanishes in an instant. Eternity is forever. It boggles the imagination.

And there is the real problem with false teachers. They divert people from the true gospel of scripture and can possibly lead them to an eternity of hell, forever cut off from God and anything good. Many will say, "Lord, lord.... Did we not do great things in your name," and they will receive the most chilling and terrifying words any soul could hear, "Depart from me. I never knew you!"

I sincerely hope that what you have read here has steered you away from counterfeit gospels and man-made Christs, and towards the real gospel; the real Jesus. His is a gospel that saves. Theirs is a fraud which cannot. God bless you as you embrace the truth!

SALVATION SCRIPTURES

Romans 10:9-10 Updated American Standard Version (UASV)

⁹ that[104] if you confess with your mouth that Jesus is Lord and believe in your heart that God raised him from the dead, you will be saved. ¹⁰ For with the heart one believes, resulting in righteousness,[105] and with the mouth one confesses, resulting in salvation.[106]

John 3:16 Updated American Standard Version (UASV)

¹⁶ For God so loved the world that he gave his only-begotten Son, in order that everyone trusting[107] in him will not be destroyed but have eternal life.

....

---

[104] Or *because*
[105] Lit *into righteousness*
[106] Lit *into salvation*
[107] Believe, faith, Trust in: (Gr. *pisteuo*) If *pisteuo os* followed by the Greek preposition eis, ("into, in among," accusative case), it is generally rendered "trusting in" or "trust in." (John 3: 16, 36; 12: 36; 14: 1) The grammatical construction of the Greek verb *pisteuo* "believe" followed by the Greek preposition eis "into" in the accusative gives us the sense of having faith into Jesus, putting faith in, trusting in Jesus. - Matt. 21: 25, 32; 27: 42; John 1:7, 12; 2: 23-24; 3: 15-16. 6:47; 11: 25; 12: 36; 14: 1; 20: 31; Acts 16: 31; Rom. 4: 3

APPENDIX 1 Partial List of Modern False Teachers;

This is by no means an exhaustive list. These are just some of the most well-known ones.

- John Avanzini - Word of Faith, Prosperity
- Heidi Baker - New Apostolic Reformation
- Jim Bakker - New Apostolic Reformation, self-appointed prophet
- Georgian Banov - New Apostolic Reformation
- Winnie Banov - New Apostolic Reformation
- Todd Bentley - New Apostolic Reformation
- Mike Bickle - New Apostolic Reformation
- William Branham - early fraudulent faith healer, deceased
- Billy Burke - Word of Faith, NAR, fraudulent faith healer
- Rodney Howard Browne - Word of Faith; known as the holy ghost bartender for imparting spiritual drunkenness
- Michael Brown - charismatic apologist, makes a career out of defending Word of Faith and New Apostolic Reformation teachers
- Juanita Bynum - Word of Faith, Prosperity, self-proclaimed prophetess
- Johnathan Cahn - Word of Faith, New Apostolic Reformation, self-proclaimed prophet
- Charles Capps - Word of Faith, deceased
- Kim Clement - New Apostolic Reformation, self-proclaimed prophet, deceased
- Todd Coontz - Word of Faith, Prosperity
- Kenneth & Gloria Copeland - Word of Faith, Prosperity
- Paul & Jan Crouch - Word of Faith, Prosperity
- Creflo & Taffy Dollar - Word of Faith, Prosperity
- Jesse Duplantis - Word of Faith, Prosperity
- Lou Engle - New Apostolic Reformation
- Steven Furtick - Word of Faith

137

- John Hagee - Word of Faith, Prosperity, denies Jesus as the Jewish Messiah

- Kenneth Hagin - Spiritual father of Word of Faith movement, deceased

- Christian Harfouche - Word of Faith, fraudulent faith healer

- Marilyn Hickey - Word of Faith

- Benny Hinn - Word of Faith, Prosperity, fraudulent faith healer

- Brian Houston - Word of Faith

- Larry & Tiz Huch - Word of Faith, Prosperity

- Cindy & Mike Jacobs - New Apostolic Reformation, self-proclaimed prophets

- TD Jakes - Word of Faith, Prosperity, Modalist (denies the Trinity)

- Leroy Jenkins - Word of Faith, fraudulent faith healer

- Bill Johnson - New Apostolic Reformation, self-proclaimed apostle, fraudulent signs and wonders, claims extra-biblical revelations

- Rick Joyner - New Apostolic Reformation, self-proclaimed prophet

- E.W. Kenyon - early proponent of incorporating New Thought and New Age ideas into Christianity, inspiration for Hagin, deceased

- Patricia King - New Apostolic Reformation, self-proclaimed prophetess

- Kathryn Kuhlman - fraudulent faith healer, deceased

- Aimee Semple McPherson - fraudulent faith healer, deceased

- Joyce Meyer - Word of Faith, Prosperity, claims extra-biblical revelations

- Myles Munroe - Word of Faith, Prosperity, deceased

- Steve Munsey - Word of Faith, Prosperity

- Mike Murdock - Word of Faith, Prosperity

- Joel Osteen - Word of Faith, Prosperity

- Rod Parsley - Word of Faith, Prosperity

- Chuck Pierce - New Apostolic Reformation

- Joseph Prince - Word of Faith, Prosperity, Hyper-grace

- James Robison - Word of Faith

- Sid Roth - New Apostolic Reformation, claims extra-biblical revelations

- R.W. Shambach - fraudulent faith healer, deceased

- Robert Tilton - Word of Faith, Prosperity

- Kris Vallotton - New Apostolic Reformation, claims extra-biblical revelations

- C. Peter Wagner - New Apostolic Reformation, self-proclaimed prophet, deceased

- Lance Wallnau - New Apostolic Reformation, self-proclaimed prophet

- Paula White - Word of Faith, Prosperity

- Todd White - New Apostolic Reformation, fraudulent faith healer

- Andrew Wommack - Word of Faith, Prosperity

APPENDIX 2: Commonly Misused Scriptures

(1) Jeremiah 29:11 Updated American Standard Version (UASV)

¹¹ "'For I know the thoughts that I am thinking toward you,' declares Jehovah, 'thoughts of peace, and not of calamity, to give you a future and a hope.

False teachers, especially in the Word of Faith / Prosperity movements, love to quote this verse as a proof text for their insistence that God wants all believers to be financially and materially prosperous. Unfortunately, this is a perfect example of taking a verse out of context and trying to make it say what they want it to say. Once again - context matters. This verse was a promise from God, that He would rescue the people of Israel from a period of Babylonian exile and restore to them all that they had lost. Is it possible that this verse has a secondary meaning as a promise to future believers? Perhaps, but there is no way to prove it by this or any other scripture.

(2) Luke 11:9 Updated American Standard Version (UASV)

⁹ And I say to you, keep on asking, and it will be given you; keep on seeking, and you will find; keep on knocking, and it will be opened to you.

Another favorite of the prosperity preachers, this verse is *not* saying that God is waiting to grant us every desire of our foolish hearts. Looked at in context, Jesus had just told his disciples what they *should* be asking for; His will to be done, the

eventual coming of His Kingdom, our daily provisions, forgiveness of sins, etc. Jesus was saying, *ask for these things* and they shall be given to you.

(3) Matthew 7:1 Updated American Standard Version (UASV)

"Do not judge so that you will not be judged"

This verse is a favorite of false teachers, whenever confronted with the unbiblical nature of their teachings. When understood in context, we are not to judge *unbelievers*, as they cannot be expected to live righteously. Other scriptures* clearly tell us that we are to judge other believers with righteous judgment, not hypocritically, and that we are to test the spirits to determine if they are of God.

John 7:24 Updated American Standard Version (UASV)

²⁴ Do not judge by appearances, but judge with righteous judgment

Titus 3:10 Updated American Standard Version (UASV)

¹⁰ Reject a divisive man after a first and second warning, 11 knowing that such a man is perverted and is sinning, being self-condemned.}

(4) 3 John 2 Updated American Standard Version (UASV)

² Beloved one, I pray that in all things you continue to prosper[108] and enjoy good health, just as your soul is prospering.

Another favorite of the health and wealth crowd, this verse is by no means saying that God wants everyone to be prosperous in a material sense. The verse itself, is a standard greeting in a first century letter; the equivalent of us writing to someone and saying, "How are you? I hope you're doing well." False teachers are rather averse to using scriptures in their intended context.

(5) Romans 8: 28 Updated American Standard Version (UASV)

²⁸ And we know that all things work together for good for those who love God, for those who are called according to his purpose.

Will God work out everything for good in our lives? If we are believers - absolutely, but not necessarily in *this life*. The Word of Faith crowd might quote this verse to someone who's just been diagnosed with cancer and mislead them into thinking they're going to be healed and all will be well. Maybe, maybe not. But when that person passes into their glorious eternity with Christ, *that's* when God will have worked *all things together for good*.

(6) Hebrews 13: 8 Updated American Standard Version (UASV)

⁸ Jesus Christ is the same yesterday and today, and forever.

Charismatics like to use this as a proof text to imply that believers today should expect to manifest the same types of miracles and other supernatural gifts as those displayed by Jesus and the Apostles. Yes, Jesus is the same as always, but does He always deal with us in the exact same ways throughout all of history? No. Is He preparing to flood the earth again? Is He still expecting us to obey the Levitical Ceremonial Laws? Is He still walking among us in human form? Does He still need to be crucified and raised from the dead again? Is He still revealing new scriptures? No.

---

[108] *Lit. to make one's way well*

Neither does He need to authenticate Himself or His Apostles with signs and wonders to establish the church. That's been done.

Joel 2:28 Updated American Standard Version (UASV)

[28] "And it will come to pass afterward, that I will pour out my Spirit on all flesh; your sons and your daughters will prophesy, your old men will dream dreams, and your young men will see visions.

The NAR use this verse to validate their claims of new, extra-biblical revelations. However, that's not what the verse is talking about. It's talking about the Day of Pentecost, which has passed. It is not describing anything we see happening in our day.

Bibliography

Akin, D. L. (2001). *The New American Commentary: 1, 2, 3 John.* Nashville, TN: Broadman & Holman .

Akin, D. L., Nelson, D. P., & Peter R. Schemm, J. (2007). *A Theology for the Church.* Nashville: B & H Publishing.

Alden, R. L. (2001). *Job, The New American Commentary, vol. 11* . Nashville: Broadman & Holman Publishers.

Anders, M. (1999). *Holman New Testament Commentary: vol. 8, Galatians-Colossians* . Nashville, TN: Broadman & Holman Publishers.

Anders, M. (2005). *Holman Old Testament Commentary - Proverbs* . Nashville: B&H Publishing.

Anders, M., & Butler, T. (2002). *Holman Old Testament Commentary: Isaiah.* Nashville, TN: B&H Publishing.

Anders, M., & Lawson, S. (2004). *Holman Old Testament Commentary - Psalms: 11.* Grand Rapids: B&H Publishing.

Anders, M., & McIntosh, D. (2009). *Holman Old Testament Commentary - Deuteronomy.* Nashville: B&H Publishing.

Anders, M., & McIntosh, D. (2009). *Holman Old Testament Commentary - Deuteronomy.* Nashville: B&H Publishing.

Andrews, E. D. (2015). *EVIDENCE THAT YOU ARE TRULY CHRISTIAN: Keep Testing Yourselves to See If You Are In the Faith - Keep Examining Yourselves.* Cambridge, OH: Christian Publishing House.

Andrews, E. D. (2016). *THE CHRISTIAN APOLOGIST: Always Being Prepared to Make a Defense [Second Edition].* Cambridge, OH: Christian Publishing House.

Andrews, E. D. (2018). *REASONABLE FAITH: Saving Those Who Doubt.* Cambridge, OH: Christian Publishing House.

Andrews, E. D. (2018). *REASONING FROM THE SCRIPTURES: Sharing CHRIST as You Help Others to Learn about the Mighty works of God.* Cambridge, Ohio: Christian Publishing House.

Andrews, E. D. (2018). *REASONING WITH THE WORLD'S VARIOUS RELIGIONS: Examining and Evangelizing Other Faiths.* Cambridge, OH: Christian Publishing House.

Andrews, S. J., & Bergen, R. D. (2009). *Holman Old Testament Commentary: 1-2 Samuel.* Nashville: Broadman & Holman.

Barker, K. L., & Bailey, W. (2001). *The New American Commentary: vol. 20, Micah, Nahum, Habakkuk, Zephaniah.* Nashville, TN: Broadman & Holman Publishers.

Benner, D. G., & Hill, P. C. (1985, 1999). *Baker Encyclopedia of Psychology and Counseling (Second Edition).* Grand Rapids: Baker Books.

Bercot, D. W. (1998). *A Dictionary of Early Christian Beliefs.* Peabody: Hendrickson.

Bergen, R. D. (1996). *The New American Commentary: 1-2 Samuel.* Nashville: Broadman & Holman.

Blomberg, C. (1992). *The New American Commentary: Matthew.* Nashville, TN: Broadman & Holman Publishers.

Boa, K., & Kruidenier, W. (2000). *Holman New Testament Commentary: Romans.* Nashville: Broadman & Holman.

Borchert, G. L. (2001). *The New American Commentary: John 1-11.* Nashville, TN: Broadman & Holman Publishers.

Borchert, G. L. (2002). *The New American Commentary vol. 25B, John 12–21.* Nashville: Broadman & Holman Publishers.

Brand, C., Draper, C., & Archie, E. (2003). *Holman Illustrated Bible Dictionary: Revised, Updated and Expanded.* Nashville, TN: Holman.

Breneman, M. (1993). *The New American Commentary, vol. 10, Ezra, Nehemiah, Esther.* Nashville: Broadman & Holman Publishers.

Brooks, J. A. (1992). *The New American Commentary: Mark (Volume 23).* Nashville: Broadman & Holman Publishers.

Butler, T. C. (2000). *Holman New Testament Commentary: Luke.* Nashville, TN: Broadman & Holman Publishers.

Butler, T. C. (2005). *Holman Old Testament Commentary - Hosea, Joel, Amos, Obadiah, Jonah, Micah.* Nashville: Broadman & Holman Publishers.

Christiaan, E. (2015). *TITHING: Exposing One Of The Biggest Lies In The Church.* New York, NY: BookPatch LLC.

Cole, R. D. (2000). *THE NEW AMERICAN COMMENTARY: Volume 3b Numbers.* Nashville: Broadman & Holman Publishers.

Cooper, L. E. (1994). *The New American Commentary, Ezekiel, vol. 17.* Nashville, TN: Broadman & Holman Publishers.

Cooper, R. (2000). *Holman New Testament Commentary: Mark.* Nashville: Broadman & Holman Publishers.

Dockery, D. S., & Butler, T. C. (1992). *Holman Bible Handbook.* Nashville, TN: Holman Bible Publishers.

Easley, K. H. (1998). *Revelation, vol. 12, Holman New Testament Commentary.* Nashville, TN:: Broadman & Holman Publishers.

Elwell, W. A. (2001). *Evangelical Dictionary of Theology (Second Edition).* Grand Rapids: Baker Academic.

Elwell, W. A., & Beitzel, B. J. (1988). *Baker Encyclopedia of the Bible.* Grand Rapids, MI: Baker Book House.

Elwell, W. A., & Comfort, P. W. (2001). *Tyndale Bible Dictionary.* Wheaton: Tyndale House Publishers.

Ferguson, E. (2005). *Church History ,Volume One: From Christ to Pre-Reformation: The Rise and Growth of the Church in Its Cultural, Intellectual, and Political Context.* Grand Rapids, MI: Zondervan.

Gamble, H. Y. (1997). *Books and Readers in the Early Church: A History of Early Christian Texts.* New Haven and London: Yale University Press.

Gangel, K. O. (1998). *Holman New Testament Commentary: Acts.* Nashville, TN: Broadman & Holman Publishers.

Gangel, K. O. (2000). *Holman New Testament Commentary, vol. 4, John.* Nashville, TN: Broadman & Holman Publishers.

Gangel, K. O. (2001). *Holman Old Testament Commentary: Daniel.* Nashville: Broadman & Holman Publishers.

Gangel, K., & Anders, M. (2002). *Daniel, vol. 18, Holman Old Testament Commentary.* Nashville, TN: Broadman & Holman Publishers.

Garrett, D. A. (1993). *Proverbs, Ecclesiastes, Song of Songs, The New American Commentary, vol. 14.* Nashville: Broadman & Holman Publishers.

Garrett, D. A. (1993). *The New American Commentary: Vol. 14 (Proverbs, Ecclesiastes, Song of Songs).* Nashville: Broadman & Holman Publishers.

George, T. (2001). *The New American Commentary: Galatians.* Nashville, TN: Broadman & Holman Publishers.

House, P. R. (2001). *The New American Commentary: 2 Kings*. Nashville: Broadman & Holman Publishers.

Larson, K. (2000). *Holman New Testament Commentary, vol. 9, I & II Thessalonians, I & II Timothy, Titus, Philemon.* Nashville, TN: Broadman & Holman Publishers.

Lea, T. D. (1999). *Holman New Testament Commentary: Hebrews, James.* Nashville, TN: Broadman & Holman Publishers.

Lea, T. D., & Griffin, H. P. (1992). *The New American Commentary, vol. 34, 1, 2 Timothy, Titus.* Nashville: Broadman & Holman Publishers.

Martin, D. M. (2001, c1995). *The New American Commentary 33 1, 2 Thessalonians*. Nashville, TN: Broadman & Holman.

Martin, G. S. (2002). *Holman Old Testament Commentary: Numbers.* Nashville: Broadman & Holman Publishers.

Mathews, K. A. (2001). *The New American Commentary vol. 1A, Genesis 1-11:26*. Nashville: Broadman & Holman Publishers.

Matthews, K. A. (2001). *The New American Commentary Vol. 1B, Genesis 11:27-50:26.* Nashville: Broadman and Holman Publishers.

Melick, R. R. (2001). *The New American Commentary: Philippians, Colossians, Philemon, electronic ed., Logos Library System.* Nashville: Broadman & Holman Publishers.

Melick, R. R. (2001). *The New American Commentary: vol. 32, Philippians, Colissians, Philemon.* Nashville, TN : Broadman & Holman Publishers.

Miller, S. R. (1994). *Daniel, vol. 18, The New American Commentary.* Nashville:: Broadman & Holman Publishers.

Mounce, R. H. (2001). *The New American Commentary: Vol. 27 Romans.* Nashville, TN: Broadman & Holman Publishers.

Mounce, R. H. (2001, c1995). *Romans: The New American Commentary 27.* Nashville: Broadman & Holman.

Mounce, W. D. (2006). *Mounce's Complete Expository Dictionary of Old & New Testament Words.* Grand Rapids, MI: Zondervan.

Polhill, J. B. (2001). *The New American Commentary 26: Acts.* Nashville: Broadman & Holman Publishers.

Pratt Jr, R. L. (2000). *Holman New Testament Commentary: I & II Corinthians, vol. 7.* Nashville: Broadman & Holman Publishers.

Richardson, K. (1997). *The New American Commentary Vol. 36 James.* Nashville: Broadman & Holman Publishers.

Robinson, D. W. (1997). *Total Church Life: How to be a First Century Chrurch.* Nashville, TN: Briadman and Holman.

Rooker, M. F. (2000). *The New American Commentary, vol. 3A, Leviticus.* Nashville: Broadman & Holman Publishers.

Rooker, M. F. (2001). *Leviticus: The New American Commentary.* Nashville: Broadman & Holman.

Rooker, M. F. (2005). *Holman Old Testament Commentary: Ezekiel.* Nashville: Broadman & Holman Publishers.

Schreiner, T. R. (2003). *The New American Commentary: 1, 2 Peter, Jude.* Nashville: Broadman & Holman.

Smith, G. (2007). *The New American Commentary: Isaiah 1-39, Vol. 15a.* Nashville, TN: B & H Publishing Group.

Smith, G. (2009). *The New American Commentary: Isaiah 40-66, Vol. 15b.* Nashville, TN: B&H Publishing.

Stein, R. H. (2001, c1992). *The New American Commentary: Luke.* Nashville, TN: Broadman & Holman .

Stuart, D. K. (2006). *The New American Commentary: An Exegetical Theological Exposition of Holy Scripture EXODUS.* Nashville: Broadman & Holman.

Swanson, J. (1997). *Dictionary of Biblical Languages with Semantic Domains: Greek (New Testament).* Oak Harbor: Logos Research Systems.

Swanson, J. (1997). *Dictionary of Biblical Languages with Semantic Domains: Hebrew (Old Testament).* Oak Harbor: Logos Research Systems.

Taylor, R. A., & Clendenen, R. E. (2007). *The New American Commentary: Haggai, Malachi, , vol. 21A .* Nashville, TN: Broadman & Holman Publishers.

Vine, W. E., Unger, M. F., & White Jr., W. (1996). *Vine's Complete Expository Dictionary of Old and New Testament Words.* Nashville, TN: T. Nelson.

Vunderink, R. W., & Bromiley, G. W. (1979–1988). *The International Standard Bible Encyclopedia, Revised (, .* Grand Rapids, MI: Wm. B. Eerdmans.

Walls, D., & Anders, M. (1996). *Holman New Testament Commentary: I & II Peter, I, II & III John, Jude.* Nashville: Broadman & Holman Publishers.

Weber, S. K. (2000). *Holman New Testament Commentary, vol. 1, Matthew.* Nashville, TN: Broadman & Holman Publishers.

Wood, D. R. (1996). *New Bible Dictionary (Third Edition).* Downers Grove: InterVarsity Press.

Woodbridge, J., & James III, F. A. (2013). *Church History, Volume Two: From Pre-Reformation to the Present Day: The Rise and Growth of the Church in Its Cultural, Intellectual, and Political Context.* Grand Rapids, MI: Zondervan.

CPSIA information can be obtained
at www.ICGtesting.com
Printed in the USA
LVHW082118220521
688243LV00013B/564